BRAIN
FOODS
for KIDS

BRAIN FOODS for KIDS

Over 100 recipes to boost
your child's intelligence

NICOLA GRAIMES

CARROLL & BROWN PUBLISHERS LIMITED

First published in 2004 in the United Kingdom by

Carroll & Brown Publishers Limited
20 Lonsdale Road
London NW6 6RD

Project Editor Caroline Smith
Art Editor Anne Fisher
Photographer Jules Selmes

Text © Nicola Graimes 2004
Illustrations and compilation © Carroll & Brown Limited 2004

A CIP catalogue record for this book is available from the British Library.

ISBN 1-903258-93-6

10987654321

Reproduced by RALI, Spain
Printed and bound in Singapore by Imago

CONTENTS

INTRODUCTION

All our children come into this world with a certain amount of intelligence. Yet, the question that fascinates me and has spurred me to research and write this book is can we, as parents, help our children improve on their inherent intelligence through a healthy diet and lifestyle?

From birth children are constantly learning new skills, from the first smile to talking, from crawling to walking and running, then on to reading and writing. Their brains need constant, good-quality nourishment to perform these functions and a whole range of other tasks. To put it into perspective, the brain represents just two per cent of body weight but demands a massive 30 per cent of the body's total energy supply.

My interest in child intelligence and behaviour has been further fuelled by the growing scientific evidence that you can enhance your child's brain-power by providing him or her with certain nutrients, and that a deficiency in just one nutrient may have a detrimental affect on behaviour and learning capabilities.

Now, this may sound straightforward but, as we all know, children can be very fickle in their tastes and eating habits. Most parents have their own methods of getting their children to eat. Mine are probably no different to many others. I know that it's best not to panic, to avoid confrontation at meal times and to avoid giving children 'junk' in place of decent meals just because they won't eat what you've given them. I've also realised that with a

little gentle persuasion and by providing children with as much variety as possible, you'll be on the right track. My daughter went through some very fussy food fads: in her eyes she had better things to do than sit down and eat a meal. But now, happily, the tables have turned and she eats most things that are put in front of her. My son seemed to be following suit, but now, rather than preparing an endless collection of dishes in the hope that he will eat something, I've relaxed, and know that he will eat if he's hungry.

Parents have a lot to contend with. Children are influenced by TV advertising for highly coloured drinks, fast food and processed snacks, by peer pressure and by the lure of the free toys offered by some manufacturers. The statistics are frightening: more children than ever are overweight (just look around the playground) and are therefore at greater risk of life-threatening conditions such as heart disease and diabetes. What's more, the social stigma of being overweight can have a seriously detrimental effect on a child's confidence.

We all want the best for our children and providing them with a good balanced diet gives them the best start in life. The following recommendations are at the heart of this book.

YOUR BRAINBOOSTING ACTION PLAN

Eating the right foods and cutting out the junk is the crucial first step towards providing the brain with the nutrients it needs for normal brain function.

The power of exercise *One recent study showed that 40–69 per cent of children are largely inactive – yet physical exercise is fundamentally important in nurturing both body and mind. Running, swimming and other aerobic exercise increases the supply of oxygenated blood to the brain, benefiting memory and attention span.*

A good start *Research has found that eating breakfast is the best way to get brain cells fired up, improving memory and concentration. A good mix of protein and carbohydrates is recommended. See page 41.*

Little and often *Children have high energy requirements relative to their size, so need energy-dense, nutritious foods in small but regular amounts. Regular meals and healthy snacks will keep blood-sugar levels steady and ensure sustained amounts of energy. See page 42.*

Fresh is best *Fruit and vegetables are crucial for good health and wellbeing, and are great sources of vital antioxidant vitamins and minerals for the brain. However, the UK National Diet and Nutrition Survey 2000 found that children eat less than half the recommended five portions of fruit and vegetables a day. See page 20.*

Fishy business *Recent studies confirm that consuming fish oils can raise IQ levels, even before birth, and they have also been shown to benefit children with dyslexia and ADHD. See page 18.*

Dump the junk *Poor quality, high-fat, high-sugar, additive-laden foods do no one any favours, unsettling blood-sugar levels and robbing the body of vital nutrients. See page 27.*

Role of iron *Studies have shown a positive link between IQ scores and iron intake, yet iron deficiency is common. Lack of iron is associated with delays in development, poor concentration, irritability, mood swings and depression. See page 17.*

Water for life *Most children don't drink enough water, favouring cans of carbonated drinks instead. Dehydration can affect concentration and intellectual performance, as well as the transportation of nutrients around the body. See page 23.*

Building
A BETTER BRAIN

Here you'll find a wealth of advice about how to enhance your child's brain power. Individual beneficial nutrients are mentioned, but it is important to recognise that any one of these should form part of an overall balanced diet and active lifestyle. The hope is that you will take on board many of the suggestions found here: long-term improvements in diet should start with our children – and the younger the better.

*Bright*BEGINNINGS

From the moment of conception itself, your child needs particular nutrients to help him or her develop healthily. So, what you eat during pregnancy is very important in making sure your baby has a healthy brain and body. By including the recommended brain foods in your diet, you can pass on their benefits to your developing baby.

A Healthy Pregnancy Diet

In terms of eating the right food, the first few weeks of pregnancy are some of the most important. However, at this stage many women won't realise that they are pregnant. So if you're planning to have a baby, it's a good idea to start eating a nutrient-rich diet before you conceive. And, if you do miss those early weeks, don't worry. Simply start to eat well once you know you are pregnant.

During the first six months of pregnancy you shouldn't need more food than usual. What is important is the quality of your diet. Pregnancy is a time to nurture both you and your baby. Eat the right foods, rich in the right nutrients, and you'll not only help your baby grow but also help yourself to enjoy a healthy pregnancy and to produce good-quality breast milk once your baby is born.

Choose fresh rather than processed foods whenever possible and eat at least five portions of fruit and vegetables a day for essential vitamins, antioxidants, minerals and fibre. Try to eat a range of different types and colours of fruit and vegetables for optimum benefit.

Substitute caffeine-free herbal teas and coffee alternatives for the real stuff.

VITAMINS

As your baby begins to grow inside you, the brain is one of his or her first organs to develop. Vital to its healthy development is an adequate supply of folic acid, one of the B vitamins. Folic acid works alongside vitamin B_{12} to form new cells and is crucial to the development of the spinal cord – inadequate supplies may result in neural tube defects or spina bifida. Therefore, women planning a baby are recommended to take a daily supplement of 400mcg of folic acid for, ideally, three months before conception and up to the twelfth week of pregnancy. Folic acid can be found in certain foods (see right) so it's also a good idea to add them to your diet to increase your intake. Folic acid is, however, easily destroyed during cooking, so lightly cook vegetables or eat them raw whenever possible.

Vitamin B$_{12}$ is also vital for the formation of red blood cells. Sources include yeast extract, meat, fish, dairy and soya products and eggs.

There is new evidence to suggest that vitamins E and C can play a role in reducing the risk of pre-eclampsia during pregnancy. This rare condition causes a severe rise in blood pressure that is dangerous to both mother and baby. Although most pregnant women won't suffer pre-eclampsia, it is wise to eat vitamin E-rich foods, such as avocados, sunflower and safflower oils, almonds and hazelnuts, and plenty of fresh fruit and vegetables high in vitamin C. Vitamin C is also important in helping you absorb the iron in your diet – a vital mineral for pregnant women.

MINERALS

During pregnancy, calcium and magnesium are vital for the developing bones and healthy nervous system of your baby. Your body will absorb calcium more efficiently at this time but make sure you include adequate amounts of dairy products in your diet. Non-dairy sources of calcium and magnesium include soya milk and green leafy vegetables, molasses, canned sardines, baked beans and sesame seeds.

Anaemia is common in pregnancy and you need enough iron to create haemoglobin, the part of the red blood cells that carries oxygen to the fetus. For the first six months after birth, babies will absorb iron from breast or formula milk, but they will also rely on iron stores in their bodies – another reason for making sure your iron intake during pregnancy is sufficient. You can get iron from foods such as red meat, dark poultry meat, eggs, leafy green vegetables, dried fruit, fortified breakfast cereals, whole grains, nuts and pulses.

ESSENTIAL FATTY ACIDS

It is important to include a good range of essential fatty acids in your diet. Oily fish is a good source of the long-chain polyunsaturated fats, DHA (Docosahexaenoic Acid) and EPA (Eicosapentaenoic Acid), essential for healthy eye and brain development. Women should ensure adequate levels prior to conception, throughout pregnancy and while breastfeeding, since 70 per cent of the cells that make up the adult brain are formed before birth. Two portions of fish are recommended per week, one of which should be oily, such as tuna, salmon, sardines, trout or mackerel.

A recent Norwegian study looked at the infants of nearly 600 women who were given

nutrient
KNOW-HOW

GOOD SOURCES OF FOLIC ACID

- Nuts & seeds
- Eggs
- Fortified breakfast cereals, wheatgerm, bread & flour
- Legumes & lentils
- Avocados
- Leafy green vegetables, such as spinach, lettuce & mustard greens
- Broccoli, Brussels sprouts, & asparagus
- Orange juice

OFF THE MENU

Liver is high in vitamin A, which can damage the developing fetus if eaten in excessive amounts.

Soft and blue-veined cheese such as Brie, Stilton and Camembert can harbour a bacteria called listeria, which may cause miscarriage or stillbirth.

Peanuts are causing increasingly greater numbers of children to suffer from allergic reactions. It is now believed that sensitivity to peanuts can start in the womb, so it is advisable to cut them out during pregnancy, particularly if there is a history of peanut allergy, hay fever, eczema or asthma in the family.

Uncooked or partially cooked eggs may harbour salmonella.

Shark, swordfish and marlin and more than two medium-sized cans of tuna or one fresh tuna steak a week should be avoided by pregnant and breastfeeding women, and those intending to conceive. This is due to the levels of mercury present in these fish, which can harm an unborn child's nervous system. The US Food and Drink Administration (FDA) also recommends avoiding tilefish and king mackerel for the same reason.

Alcohol depletes zinc levels and can cross the placenta, causing birth defects if taken in excess. To be on the safe side, cut it out altogether.

Caffeine also can cross the placenta and drinking excessive amounts (more than 6 cups a day) has been linked to nerve abnormalities and low birth weight. Pregnant women are now recommended to limit the amount of caffeine they consume to no more than 300mg a day (see opposite). Caffeine is found in tea, coffee, some carbonated drinks and chocolate. Tea interferes also with iron absorption.

an omega-3 supplement from 18 weeks of pregnancy to three months after birth. Researchers looked at the cognitive performance of the breastfed infants from birth up until age four and concluded that the supplement seemed to enhance mental development in the children.

Eggs (thoroughly cooked), walnuts and linseeds also provide omega-3 fatty acids, while the equally vital omega-6, which assists in normal nerve function, is found in nuts, seeds and their oils.

CHOLINE

To have a good memory, your child's brain needs the neurotransmitter acetylcholine, a deficiency of which is probably the most common cause of memory decline. It is derived from the nutrient choline, which is found particularly in egg yolks, grains, nuts, beans and fish such as sardines. Vitamins B_1, B_5, B_{12} and C as well as lecithin are also essential for the formation of acetylcholine.

SUPPLEMENTS

If you've suffered with severe morning sickness or if your diet is poor, it may be wise to consider a specially formulated vitamin and mineral supplement for pregnant women. This can give you a good balance of nutrients, including betacarotene (the plant version of vitamin A, which is not recommended in large amounts), zinc, iron, magnesium and calcium, which are important for the developing fetus and can help with muscle cramps.

The Early Months

Once your baby is born, there's no doubt that breastfeeding is the best start you can give your child. Your breast milk contains everything your baby needs in just the right quantities. It is rich in protein, minerals (including iron and calcium) and vitamins A, D and B_{12}. Current recommendations from the World Health Organisation advise mothers to feed their babies on breast milk alone until they are at least six months old. Breast milk also boosts immunity, protects against the risk of gastroenteritis and ear and respiratory infections, asthma and eczema.

POST-PREGNANCY DIET

Nursing mothers are advised to consume 450kcal more than the average daily recommendation of 2000kcal as you will need extra energy and nutrients. However, you will use up some of the stores laid down in pregnancy while breastfeeding, which may go some way towards returning you to a pre-pregnancy weight. The recommendations on the preceding pages should be followed to ensure your baby receives an adequate supply of nutrients including the essential fatty acids and choline. Some of these substances are naturally present in breast milk but your diet can also play an important role.

BREAST MILK AS BRAIN FOOD

Breast milk is vital to the development of your child's brain and central nervous system as it contains crucial fatty acids, including omega-3 and 6, which can positively affect cognitive development. Recent research also shows that breastfeeding can help improve a child's long-term intelligence. Breastfed babies tend to have higher IQs than formula-fed babies. Additionally, researchers at an American university believe it may be possible for breastfeeding mothers to permanently enhance the memories of their babies. This is due to the nutrient choline, which is found in breast milk, particularly in the first few days after birth. It is believed that choline is of critical importance in 'memory development, the determination of adult memory capacity and resistance to age-related memory impairments'.

FORMULA MILK

While it is widely acknowledged that breast milk is the best for a baby's development, formula milk manufacturers have been working hard to improve the nutritional status of their products. It is not always possible for some women to breastfeed, and these mothers should not feel guilty about bottle feeding. Formula milk is made to strict guidelines and manufacturers try to ensure it resembles breast milk as closely as possible. Some are even fortifying milk with the essential fatty acids linked to improving memory and IQ; however, studies suggest that these are not so readily absorbed compared to those in breast milk.

*Brain*NUTRIENTS

For good health and optimum brainpower, a child's diet should contain the 'proper' amounts of certain nutrients. Balance and variety are the key and a deficiency in just one vital nutrient can impair cognitive performance.

nutrient
KNOW-HOW

FIBRE

Although essential to keep a mature digestive system working correctly, children aged under five should not be given too many unrefined whole grains and cereals. Babies and young children can find fibre difficult to digest in large quantities. They may become full before they have eaten the variety of foods needed for a balanced diet. Instead, offer a balance of refined and unrefined starchy foods.

CARBOHYDRATES

The brain needs a constant and steady supply of glucose, which supplies it with the energy it needs. Carbohydrate foods, and preferably complex carbohydrates, are the best sources, and should make up about a third of a child's diet.

Carbohydrates comes in two forms: simple (also known as sugars) and complex (starches). Sugars are either intrinsic, such as those already present in fruit, or extrinsic, such as refined sugar added to sweets, cakes and biscuits.

The carbohydrates in your child's diet should be made up principally of intrinsic sugars and unrefined complex carbohydrates found in whole-grain bread, potatoes, pulses, wholemeal pasta, brown rice and vegetables. Unrefined carbohydrates are preferable to refined because they are higher in nutrients and fibre and, crucially for the brain, they help to keep blood-sugar levels steady, so providing long-term, sustained energy.

Refined sugary foods lead to a surge in blood-sugar levels, which can be followed by a slump. Your child's concentration and attention span will wane and he or she will become fatigued. Extreme highs and lows in blood-sugar levels can result in dizziness, irritability and mood swings (see also page 26).

PROTEIN

We actually need relatively small amounts of protein (children aged 4–10 need between 15–28 grams per day), but variety is important to get the full spectrum of the different nutrients found in protein foods. Protein is found in both animal (meat, poultry, eggs and dairy produce) and plant sources (beans, lentils, nuts and seeds).

Protein is made up of 25 amino acids. Eight of these are known as essential amino acids because they have to be provided by diet and are not made in the body. Among their many roles, amino acids are crucial for making neurotransmitters, the brain's messengers, and so are vital to brain chemistry and emotions. The amino acid tyrosine, found in fish, dairy products, eggs, oats and turkey can lift mood and increase alertness, while another amino acid, phenylalanine, is used to regulate blood sugar through insulin.

Proteins are said to satisfy the appetite for longer than carbohydrates, yet the latter are believed to provide long-term energy. Ironically, many foods are a combination of the two.

FAT

The brain is comprised of 60 per cent fat, which has to come from the diet. The type of fat your child eats, therefore, affects the composition of the fats in his or her brain. This is why it is so important to include the 'right' types of fat in your child's diet, as these are essential for brain development and enable children to think and to store and retrieve memories.

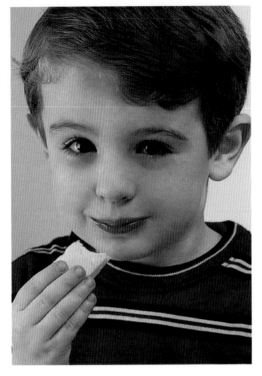

The most useful group of fats for brain and eye function are the long-chain polyunsaturated fatty acids, including omega-3 fats, EPA and DHA, but these are also the ones children (and adults) are least likely to get from their diets. A deficiency in omega-3 is said to be one of the major causes of degenerative disease and of a corresponding decline in brain function. There also appears to be a correlation between fatty acid levels in infants and their intellectual and behavioural performance as children.

You will find the richest amounts of omega-3 in oily fish (see page 18) but it also is available in eggs and some plant foods. However, these are not as potent as those found in fish oils.

The other essential fatty acid is omega-6, found in plant sources, such as nuts and seeds, as well as corn, safflower and sunflower oils. Phospholipids, other fatty-acid substances found particularly in eggs, fish and soya, are needed for brain cell membrane repair and the transmission of electrical nerve impulses.

Bad fats, including saturated as well as hydrogenated or trans fats, have a negative effect on the brain. Once the hydrogenated fat gets into the cell walls, it interferes with the assimilation of nutrients, resulting in toxic build-up. Unfortunately, it is very easy for children to eat too many 'bad' fats, especially if their diets are made up mainly of highly processed or fast foods. Hydrogenated fat is found in a wide range of manufactured foods from margarine, sausages and salad dressings to pies, biscuits and cakes. Fortunately, some major food producers are now attempting to reduce (or even eliminate) the hydrogenated fat content of their products.

VITAMINS & MINERALS

Brain function is influenced by a variety of essential vitamins and minerals, and pound for pound a child needs a lot more than the average adult. Vitamins and minerals also are crucial for the production of energy, boosting the immune system, the nervous system and practically every body process.

Vitamins A, C and E are antioxidants that protect the brain and body from toxins and pollution. Vitamin C is essential for a healthy immune system and for turning food into mental and physical energy. It also helps us to absorb iron.

B vitamins are vital for brain function, a healthy nervous system and energy metabolism. They are important in the production of the brain neurotransmitters (messengers) dopamine, adrenaline, noradrenaline and serotonin. Poor concentration and memory, lack of energy, insomnia and irritability are signs of possible deficiency.

Calcium and magnesium are known as nature's tranquillisers, since they relax nerve and muscle cells. A lack of these minerals can make children feel nervous, irritable and aggressive. A deficiency of choline, a vitamin-like compound, has been linked to possible memory and thought impairment. Along with lecithin and the B vitamins, choline enables the body to produce acetylcholine, which transmits electrical impulses to the brain and nervous system. Zinc is crucial for memory and brain function. It is also said to be important in the synthesis of the brain-calming chemical, serotonin. Boron has been found to aid memory, improve attention and mental alertness and is essential for energy metabolism.

Iron has many functions in the body, one of which is to carry oxygen in the blood. Deficiency can make children feel tired and irritable and less able to concentrate, as well as affecting their development. Numerous studies have found that there are a great number of children (and adults) throughout the world lacking in this vital brain nutrient. Increasing iron consumption can lift mood and reduce anger, while an American study has linked higher intake of iron with a reduction in depression in teenage girls.

Research has also been conducted to see if there is a link between iron in the diet and IQ, and some of these studies have shown a possible positive link between IQ scores and sufficient iron intake. Iron from animal sources is better absorbed than that from plant sources, but drinking a glass of orange juice with an iron-rich meal will help encourage absorption.

Selenium is a powerful antioxidant that can protect the brain from heavy metals such as lead, used in pipes, and mercury, part of the amalgam used in some dental fillings. Even small amounts of heavy metals can accumulate in the tissues and interfere with the chemistry of the brain. Chromium helps in the control of blood-glucose levels.

VITAL VITAMINS & MINERALS, AND WHERE TO FIND THEM

Vitamin E *Nuts and seeds and their oils*

Vitamin A *Animal foods including dairy, meat, fish and eggs (as retinol) and in fruit and vegetables (as betacarotene)*

Vitamin C *Kiwi & citrus fruit, berries, green vegetables, tomatoes & peppers*

B vitamins *Whole grains, eggs, green vegetables, brown rice, meat, fish, pulses, nuts and seeds*

Calcium *Dairy products, almonds, apricots, seeds, sardines and green leafy vegetables*

Magnesium *Soya beans, whole grains, nuts, dried fruit, green leafy vegetables and meat*

Choline *Egg yolk, sardines, liver, nuts, pulses and grains*

Zinc *Brown turkey meat, shellfish, beans and wholegrains*

Boron *Nuts, apples, broccoli, peas, grapes and pulses*

Iron *Red meat, molasses, cocoa powder, parsley, eggs, pulses, green vegetables, liver, shellfish, fortified breakfast cereals*

Selenium *Whole grains, cereals, tuna, shellfish, liver, dairy products and eggs*

Chromium *Red meat, eggs, cheese, seafood, whole grains*

*Brain*FOODS

Your child's mind needs nurturing and nourishment like any other part of his or her body. Just as a good diet helps maintain a healthy heart, lungs and digestion, so it can influence the efficiency of the brain's chemical processes, improving memory, concentration and mental energy. While there are some foods that can be accused of being bad for brain function (see Brain Drain, page 26), there are many that can help children maximise their learning capability.

nutrient
KNOW-HOW

GOOD SOURCES OF OMEGA-3

- Mackerel
- Tuna
- Sardines
- Pilchards
- Herring
- Salmon (preferably wild or organic)
- Anchovies
- Trout
- Sturgeon
- Small amounts in white fish and shellfish

NON-FISH SOURCES
- Walnuts
- Linseeds (or flaxseed)
- Rapeseed
- Pumpkin seeds
- Eggs
- Soya beans

FISH & SHELLFISH

It is now widely recognised that fish and shellfish are great brain food – it's not just an old wives' tale! They contain the beneficial essential fatty acid, omega-3, along with other vitamins, minerals and amino acids. Found in the richest amounts in oily fish, omega-3 fatty acids DHA and EPA have been shown to be essential for the health and development of nerves, eyes and brain function. (The old favourite, cod-liver oil, is not the best source of essential oils for children since any pollutants tend to be stored in a fish's liver.)

These fatty acids are not produced in the body and so have to be supplied by diet. There is widespread concern that modern diets do not contain enough omega-3 fats, a lack of which

Wonder food?

FISH- AND PLANT-OIL SUPPLEMENTS

A recent study found that giving children fish- and plant-oil supplements over a three-month period had impressive results. Head teachers in a particular area were asked to select children who had shown slight difficulties in learning, memory and concentration. Half were given the supplements and the other half a placebo. Over 40 per cent of those taking the supplements improved their scores in intelligence tests, and demonstrated improvements in reading age and numeracy. Research also shows that the Japanese, who eat a lot of fish, have, on average, IQ's 6 per cent higher than the average American.

nutrient
KNOW-HOW

GOOD SOURCES OF COMPLEX CARBOHYDRATES

- Whole grain wheat
- Brown rice
- Wild rice
- Millet
- Buckwheat
- Quinoa
- Barley
- Oats
- Rye

has been linked to poor concentration and memory, dyslexia, behavioural problems, learning difficulties as well as hyperactivity in some sensitive children.

Children particularly need omega-3 fatty acids for their rapidly developing brains, eyes and nerves. Omega-3 has also been shown to improve mood and can help with feelings of depression. One serving of oily fish a week is recommended (but a supplement that contains a blend of omega-3 and 6 may be necessary for therapeutic purposes). Canned fish, though still beneficial, contains lower levels of omega-3 than fresh. Shark, swordfish and marlin have also been found to contain significant amounts of mercury, and the Food Standards Agency (FSA) in the UK advises that children should avoid eating these types of fish.

Fish is also a good source of choline – a nutrient needed (along with lecithin and B vitamins) to produce the brain chemical acetylcholine, vital for the rapid functioning of memory and improved learning ability. Shellfish is a good source of zinc, a crucial brain mineral for memory and concentration. Studies have shown that even a mild deficiency of zinc can impair mental function, leading to irritability, mood swings and loss of appetite; when levels are replenished memory has been found to improve. Seafood also contains the amino acid tyrosine, which has been linked to increased mental energy and alertness, along with useful amounts of B vitamins, which are vital for energy production.

GRAINS & CEREALS

Children are particularly susceptible to the effects of fluctuating blood-sugar levels; extreme highs and lows can lead to feelings of anxiety, light headedness, irritability, poor concentration and memory. Whole grains are the most nutritious option and, as complex carbohydrates, they are the body's main source of sustained energy. They also are good sources of all the key brain vitamins and minerals such as B vitamins, zinc, magnesium, folic acid, iron, selenium and vitamin E. When refined as in white flour, pasta and rice, grains and cereals lose many of their nutrients and also have an unsettling effect on blood-sugar levels.

Complex carbohydrates help to boost levels of serotonin, the brain-calming, mood-enhancing chemical. A meal containing pasta,

Did you know?

PORTION SIZE

The World Health Organisation now recommends that children eat five portions of fruit and vegetables a day – three portions of fruit and two of vegetables. But what is a portion of fruit or vegetables? Generally speaking, it is the amount a child can roughly fit into his or her hand. A glass of fresh fruit juice and a helping of beans both count as single portions.

rice, noodles, or couscous may help children to wind down – ideal at the end of the day or if your child is very active or is a bad sleeper.

FRUIT & VEGETABLES

Fruit and vegetables provide an abundance of brain nutrients, particularly antioxidants and phytochemicals, a group of natural substances that have a range of therapeutic properties. Fruit and vegetables also contain a wide range of vitamins and minerals, and since increased vitamin and mineral intake has been found to improve IQ levels, particularly in children with a poor diet, it is vital to encourage your child to eat up his or her fruit and vegetables. Three portions of fruit and two of vegetables a day are recommended.

Fruit is a good source of vitamin C, boron, selenium and carotenoids, while vegetables provide iron, vitamin C, calcium, selenium, B vitamins, magnesium, zinc and boron.

Boron is responsible for producing positive brain waves, increasing alertness and improving memory and concentration. Vitamin C aids the absorption of iron, which has been found to improve IQ and helps to energise the mind.

Numerous studies have shown that most children do not get enough fresh fruit and vegetables. It can be a struggle to get a child to 'eat up his or her greens' – a struggle that most parents have experienced.

Easy ways to increase your child's consumption

One way round this problem is to offer your child a range of different fruit and vegetables. The greater choice he or she has, the more chance there is of finding something your child really likes!

Try presenting fruit and vegetables in different ways. For example, children often will find sticks of raw vegetables more interesting and more palatable than cooked. Also, they can eat them with their hands rather than a boring knife and fork. Sticks also are good for dipping; serve them with a nutritious dip and you'll have twice the benefit.

If your children balk at the sight of certain vegetables, then you can incorporate some, such as carrots, cabbage, sweet potato, peas or even onion, into mashed potato or rösti. And if the going gets really tough, disguise puréed vegetables in sauces, soups, pies or stews.

If the amount of fruit and vegetables you can get into your child is limited, then try to make sure it is as nutritious as possible. Buy the freshest you can – ideally organic, locally grown

Creating calm

The brain-chemical serotonin has a mood-enhancing, calming effect and can induce sleepiness. Certain protein foods (turkey, chicken, eggs, lean meat, milk, cheese and soya beans) contain the amino acid tryptophan, which is needed to produce serotonin. However, levels of serotonin depend upon how efficiently tryptophan is delivered to the brain. Peak levels of tryptophan may not reach the brain because other amino acids in the same foods compete against each other. However, carbohydrate foods (such as pasta or potatoes) eaten at the same time ease the path for the tryptophan to enter the brain cells and so raise serotonin levels.

This theory suggests that a meal based on carbohydrate foods accompanied by a moderate amount of protein can help to prepare the body for sleep. Conversely, a high-protein meal with a small amount of carbohydrate may have the opposite effect, keeping us alert. This is why a meal with a higher ratio of protein to carbohydrate is seen by some nutritionists as being better for breakfast and lunch as it fuels the brain and stimulates the mind, while the ratio should be reversed for the evening meal. Other nutritionists, however, recommend that carbohydrate foods should always take pride of place on a plate.

produce – and make sure you don't keep it for too long before it's eaten. Steaming rather than boiling will help to preserve key brain nutrients.

NUTS & SEEDS

Just a handful of nuts and seeds can boost levels of B vitamins, iron, magnesium, calcium, vitamin E, selenium, potassium, zinc and omega-6 essential fatty acids, important nutrients for brain function and energy production. Children who are lacking in the B vitamins may feel tired, lethargic and have trouble maintaining concentration. Nuts and seeds also are excellent sources of protein but some varieties, such as peanuts, are high in saturated fat so should be eaten in moderation. Not only do nuts make a nutritious snack but you also can use them to give a healthy boost to casseroles, stews, desserts and cakes.

In Chinese medicine, walnuts are known as the 'longevity fruit' and are an excellent brain food since they contain both omega-3 and omega-6 essential fatty acids (EFAs). Pumpkin seeds also include both types of EFA, while Brazil nuts, and sunflower and sesame seeds and their oils are particularly rich in omega-6 fatty acids. Almonds, Brazil nuts, cashews and hazelnuts are a good source of B vitamins. Buy unsalted nuts and those that are as fresh as you can find, preferably in their shells, since they can become rancid if stored for too long. Keep them fresh in an airtight container, away from the light.

OFF THE MENU

Nuts can be the cause of a severe allergy with life-threatening symptoms. If there is any history of nut allergy within your family, consult your doctor before giving nuts to your child. Children under five should not be given whole nuts due to the risk of choking.

BEANS, PULSES & LENTILS

Excellent store-cupboard essentials, beans, pulses and lentils are often neglected at meal-times – with the exception of baked beans, of course! If you find the prospect of all that overnight soaking off-putting, canned varieties make useful alternatives but do choose those without added sugar and salt and make sure you rinse them before use.

Beans, pulses and lentils are a valuable low-fat combination of protein and carbohydrates that also provide a good mix of mind- and memory-enhancing minerals, including B vitamins, calcium, iron, magnesium, manganese and zinc. Tests have shown that children who eat adequate amounts of B vitamins will perform better in memory tests. Beans, pulses and lentils are not classified as complete proteins but including nuts and grains in the diet will ensure your child gets all the essential amino acids his or her body and mind need. Soya beans are an exception to the rule since, like meat and eggs, they are complete proteins. What's more, they also provide valuable omega-3 fats. Tofu, tempeh and miso are all made from soya beans.

Containing protein, carbohydrates, and several essential vitamins and minerals, beans, pulses and lentils are tasty and versatile brain foods.

DAIRY FOODS

Cheese, milk, yogurt and eggs are key protein foods, which are made up of essential amino acids, the building blocks of good health and mental vitality. Nevertheless, the saturated fat content of butter and cheese means that these should be eaten in moderation, since, in the long-term, they can clog the arteries that feed the brain. Dairy products are a good source of calcium and vitamins A and B. The brain-boosting amino acid tyrosine, which is converted into noradrenaline and dopamine, is found in milk and cheese and has been found to increase mental alertness and motivation. However, a milky drink at bedtime can be sleep inducing as the natural sugars in the milk (lactose) help to convert the tryptophan in the milk protein into the brain-calming substance, serotonin. Children over two years of age can be given semi-skimmed milk providing they are eating a well-balanced diet.

EGGS

Both nutritious and convenient, eggs provide lecithin, B vitamins, iron and zinc, a powerful brain combo. You also can now buy eggs from hens whose feed has been fortified with omega-3 fatty acids, which could be useful if

your offspring dislike fish. However, these do not come from free-range hens. Eggs are complete proteins, and so provide all the essential amino acids necessary to build neuro-transmitters, the brain's messengers. They are also rich in tryptophan, needed to make the brain chemical serotonin, which calms the mind and acts as a sleep inducer.

MEAT & POULTRY

Animal proteins are classified as complete proteins, meaning that they contain all the eight essential amino acids. These are required to make key neurotransmitters in the brain, believed to aid clarity of thought, concentration and vitality. Red meat is an excellent source of iron and studies have found that children are often deficient in this vital mineral, which can influence behaviour and development. Increasing consumption of iron-rich foods has been found to lift mood, reduce anger and improve IQ. Meat is also a good source of zinc, which along with iron, helps to counteract the effect of lead in the body (a 1997 UK Government report estimated that 10 per cent of children have high enough blood lead levels to impair IQ). The downside is that red meat contains saturated fat, so cut off all visible fat and only eat red meat in moderate amounts.

Poultry is a low-fat source of protein (as long as the skin is removed) and is also a good source of the amino acid tryptophan, important for the production of the brain-calming chemical serotonin. By eating a carbohydrate-based food at the same time you will encourage the passage of tryptophan into the brain. Zinc is also found in chicken and turkey.

WATER

Most children don't drink enough fluids, especially while they are at school, but decent hydration is just as important for concentration, clarity of thought and energy as a good balanced diet. A 2 per cent loss in body fluids, for example, can cause a 20 per cent reduction in both physical and mental performance. Choose from filtered or bottled water, diluted fresh fruit juice or milk and avoid carbonated sugary drinks. The amount of fluid a child needs depends on age and weight but, as a rough guide, the average 4–6-year-old should drink around five glasses a day and a 7–10-year-old should drink about six. A child who does not drink enough may experience headaches, lethargy, poor concentration and constipation. Dehydration also affects the body's ability to transport essential nutrients throughout the body and brain.

Lethargy, headaches, poor concentration and constipation are a few of the problems children can experience if their fluid intake is too low.

I can see a rainbow

Tomatoes

The greater the variety of fruit and vegetables your child eats, the wider range of nutrients he or she will get. Make a game of choosing fruit and vegetables from the various colour groups below and try to offer them in different guises: raw, steamed or stir-fried, or in stews, sauces or soups.

RED

Tomatoes, strawberries, sweet peppers, raspberries, redcurrants, apples, grapes, watermelon, cherries, radishes, rhubarb

ORANGE

Carrots, sweet peppers, pumpkin, swede, squash, sweet potato, oranges, clementines, melon, nectarines, apricots

Pumpkin

YELLOW

Bananas, courgettes, sweet peppers, marrow, beansprouts, sweetcorn, pineapple, plums

GREEN

Broccoli, Brussels sprouts, cabbage, green beans, avocado, apples, pears, salad leaves, spinach, peas, kiwi fruit

Avocado

Sweet peppers

PURPLE

Berries, aubergine, figs, plums, beetroot, red cabbage

Strawberries

Watermelon

Oranges

Peaches

Bananas

Grapes

Apples

Peas

Aubergine

Blueberries

Red cabbage

*Brain*DRAIN

Most parents are aware that diet plays an important role in their child's health. But it may come as a surprise to learn that a poor diet, lacking in nutrients, can be as bad for a child's mind as it is for his or her body. Without well-balanced and regular meals, the brain cannot work to its best ability and attention span, memory and learning capabilities all suffer. A diet based on poor-quality burgers, chicken nuggets, chips, crisps, sweets, biscuits and fizzy drinks will not provide children with the nutrients they need for healthy, active minds and bodies.

Did you know?

SUGAR ON LABELS

Sugar comes in various guises but all have a similar effect on blood-sugar levels. Sucrose, fructose, glucose, corn syrup, invert sugar and dextrose, are basically alternative names for refined sugar. Don't be tempted by labels promising 'low-sugar' where manufacturers have replaced the sugar with artificial sweeteners such as aspartame or saccharin. These have been linked with hyperactivity in children and can cause diarrhoea.

SUGAR

One of the main culprits of 'brain drain' is the refined sugar found in processed foods such as sweets, cakes, biscuits and sweetened breakfast cereals. Refined sugar has little or no nutritional value and has even been found to 'cloud' the brain when eaten in large quantities, not to mention the effect it has on tooth decay and weight gain. Highs and lows in blood-sugar levels affect both mind and body. Eating a sugary food leads to a temporary surge in blood-glucose levels, resulting in a rush of energy (think of kids after a birthday tea) that is promptly followed by a slump or sugar-low (remember those tears and tantrums as they leave the party). It is this fluctuation that is said to produce an inconsistent supply of energy to the brain, leading to poor concentration and attention span, irritability and fatigue.

Honey, molasses and maple syrup also are forms of concentrated sugar so have the same effect on blood-sugar levels, although molasses is rich in certain minerals, and honey is believed to have some therapeutic properties.

Conversely, some researchers have found that sugar has a sedative effect. This may be because as a fast-releasing carbohydrate it stimulates the production of serotonin in the brain, making us feel drowsy a couple of hours after eating.

Sugary foods often include a fair amount of fat – just think of doughnuts, biscuits and chocolate bars. Fat takes a while to digest so can make brain function sluggish. In the long-term, it also 'furs' up the arteries, restricting blood flow to the brain.

Consuming large amounts of sugar also may inhibit the assimilation of certain nutrients, suppress the immune system and lead to glucose intolerance, which means the body has problems regulating blood-sugar levels. The symptoms include irritability, depression, crying spells, fatigue, poor concentration and insomnia.

WHAT'S THE ALTERNATIVE?

Most children naturally will prefer sweet foods – to start with, breast milk is sweet – yet if eaten in moderation and as part of an overall well-balanced diet, this needn't be a problem. The main thing is to try and avoid over-processed sugary confections. Rather than cutting out sugar completely, which could lead to kids bingeing on sweets whenever they get the opportunity, you can offer some healthier alternatives (see box, right). These will still influence blood-sugar levels but in most cases, these foods will also contain fibre and some protein to buffer the impact, as well as being good sources of vitamins and minerals.

JUNK FOODS

Admittedly, the definition of junk food is hazy but it generally applies to highly processed, nutritionally deficient foods that are usually high in sugar, sweeteners, additives or fat. It would be difficult, if not nigh on impossible, to remove all manufactured foods from our children's diets but it is worth remembering that in the refining process many vitamins and minerals are destroyed that are vital for good brain health. Even when nutrients are artificially replaced, such as in breakfast cereals and breads, it is debatable whether they can be absorbed efficiently by the body.

Not only are most junk foods lacking in nutritional value, they are likely to contain artificial colours, preservatives, flavourings, salt and sugar. They also tend to be high in saturated and hydrogenated fats, or 'trans' fats. These slow down digestion, circulation and mental processes and clog the arteries, increasing the risk of diseases like heart disease and cancer.

Healthy treats

- *Fresh or dried fruits. The portion-sized bags of dried apricots, dates or raisins are convenient for trips or lunch boxes*

- *Small amounts of good-quality chocolate made with cocoa butter*

- *Flapjacks, fruit cakes, biscuits or cookies made with whole grains*

- *Fresh fruit smoothies and milk shakes*

- *Fruit bread, teacakes or muffins made with wholemeal flour and topped with cream cheese*

- *Home-made popcorn*

- *Home-made or good quality cakes*

- *Oatcakes with high-fruit, no-added sugar jam*

- *Real fruit yogurts or fromage frais, or plain yogurt that you can flavour with home-made fruit purées or a spoonful of organic honey*

CAFFEINE

As well as being found in coffee and tea, caffeine is also found in chocolate – a bar can contain up to 50 mg – and some carbonated drinks, like cola. Caffeine is a stimulant and diuretic and can cause mood swings since it affects the body's ability to control blood-sugar

OFF THE MENU

- Mass-produced, poor quality pizza, burgers and sausages
- Processed cheese slices and 'strings'
- Sliced meats with high-water, high-fat and preservative content
- Breaded chicken or fish nuggets with low meat or fish content
- Poor quality, high-fat pies and sausage rolls
- High-sugar breakfast cereals
- Highly flavoured crisps and reconstituted potato products
- Carbonated, sugary drinks such as cola and fruit-flavoured drinks, or fruit drinks rather than fresh fruit juice
- Diet versions of drinks that contain artificial sweeteners
- Highly coloured sweets containing artificial colours and gelatine
- Poor quality ice cream and highly coloured ice lollies
- Poor quality artificially flavoured yogurts
- High-sugar cereal bars or additive-laden, high-fat and high-sugar cakes and biscuits

CARBONATED DRINKS

Consumption of sweet, fizzy drinks is on the increase, yet there is nothing positive that can be said about most of them, with their added sugar, colours, sweeteners, caffeine and preservatives. Recent research in the UK found that 21 per cent of 7–10-year-olds consume nearly ten cans of fizzy drinks a week. Fizzy drinks also are high in the mineral phosphorus, which inhibits calcium absorption. Calcium is vital for the production of the brain's messengers, neurotransmitters, which are said to have an effect on emotions.

ADDITIVES & PRESERVATIVES

A number of substances are routinely added to manufactured food to enhance taste, texture and appearance or to prolong shelf life. According to research, additives may adversely affect one in seven children. Babies and young children are said to be especially vulnerable since their systems are immature and they are more exposed to them. While not all additives are potentially harmful, some of them have been linked to hyperactivity in sensitive children as well as being the potential cause of allergies, poor memory, depression and mood swings. Most additives and preservatives are listed on food labels as a capital E followed by a number, but a backlash against E numbers a few years ago has led to some manufacturers dropping this system altogether, giving the E number a name instead.

Avoiding additives altogether can be a minefield. The majority of crisp manufacturers, for example, routinely add E621 or monosodium glutamate (MSG) to flavoured

levels. One study carried out by researchers at the University of Bristol found that caffeine does not benefit mental performance in the long-term. Primary-school children who were regularly given a cup of tea in the morning began to wake up feeling groggy and tired, were generally slower and began to 'need' a cup of tea in the morning – in the way that some adults do – to make their bodies and brains feel more alert and ready for the day. Caffeine also depletes the body of certain B vitamins, zinc, potassium, calcium and iron, all vital for good all-round cognitive performance.

varieties. This flavour enhancer has been linked to 'Chinese restaurant syndrome', the symptoms of which are dizziness, anxiety, thirst and mood swings.

The orange food colouring tartrazine (E102) is just one of the many additives known to influence behaviour and possibly to trigger the symptoms of ADHD (see page 30). Others include Sunset yellow (E110), Erythrosine (E127), Benzoic acid (E219), Sodium benzoate (E211), Carmoisine (122) and Ponceau 4R (E124) as well as the previously mentioned MSG. The antioxidants BHA (E320) and BHT (E321) are also known to cause problems. A study carried out in Australia in 1994 found that 55 per cent of children in their research who responded positively to the elimination of all food dyes and additives in their diet, reacted negatively when given a single dye, such as tartrazine, again. The children were more irritable, restless and had sleep problems.

Many governments are dismissive of the case against additives, claiming that the evidence is contradictory and largely anecdotal, yet many parents who have cut out additives from their children's diets can counter this. Take, for example, the case of Michael and Christopher Parker, five-year-old identical twins. Michael was not allowed to eat snacks with dyes or preservatives for two weeks. He became noticeably calmer than his brother who continued to eat his normal diet. Michael also appeared to show a 15-point increase in IQ over the period. When the study was extended to classmates, 57 per cent of parents said that their children's behaviour had improved.

Try to avoid foods containing additives, colourings and preservatives. If you are concerned that your child reacts adversely to food additives, keep a food diary and monitor his or her behaviour over a period of time before contacting a doctor or dietitian.

(see page 30)

See page 17

Did you know? ● ● ●

THE ROLE OF ADDITIVES

ANTIOXIDANTS (E300–321) prevent food turning rancid

COLOURINGS (E100–180) add or intensify colour (some are banned in UK and US)

EMULSIFIERS, STABILIZERS, THICKENERS AND GELLING AGENTS (E322–495) affect the texture of food and bind ingredients together

FLAVOUR ENHANCERS (E620–635) enhance the flavour or smell of a food without adding any of their own

PRESERVATIVES (E200–283) prevent and slow down deterioration in food. Any processed food with a long shelf life is likely to include preservatives

---

HEAVY METALS AND PESTICIDES

Heavy metals such as lead, cadmium, mercury and aluminium accumulate in the brain and have been linked to reduced intelligence, concentration, memory and impulse control. Mercury fillings have also been linked to brain toxicity. Foods rich in zinc and selenium have been found to detoxify heavy metals in the body. See page 17 for good sources of these minerals.

The ultimate consequences of long-term exposure to pesticide residues is unknown but there is some evidence to suggest that in sensitive children pesticides may be linked to hyperactivity and allergies.

*Food*INTOLERANCES

One in ten children is thought to be affected by hyperactivity, also known as Attention Deficit Hyperactive Disorder (ADHD), which may be aggravated by poor diet, while many children suffer intolerances or allergies to particular foods.

BEHAVIOURAL PROBLEMS

The influence of diet on behaviour is somewhat controversial but poor diet, lack of essential fatty acids and food allergies can certainly exacerbate symptoms. Symptoms include destructive behaviour, restlessness, poor concentration, learning difficulties, clumsiness, irritability and poor social skills. For example, it has been suggested that children with ADHD often have problems with metabolising sugar, the symptoms of which can be more pronounced in the morning when sugary foods are eaten on an empty stomach. When sugar is refined, it is also robbed of any mineral content, particularly chromium which is needed to metabolise sugar and control blood glucose levels. This deficiency may cause bouts of hypoglycaemia leading to aggressive outbursts.

Deficiencies in zinc, calcium and magnesium can cause restlessness, poor concentration and learning difficulties and a lack of these minerals also has been linked to children with ADHD.

Vitally important are the essential fatty acids omega-3 and 6. Numerous studies have shown that a deficiency in these fatty acids can lead to behavioural problems and learning difficulties, and many children with ADHD have been found to have low levels of essential fatty acids. Research has found that boys are more likely to suffer from severe fatty acid deficiency and poorer reading and spelling abilities. Another study, still in its early stages, has linked depression and mood swings to omega-3 deficiency. Scientists suggest that these fatty acids may be able to suppress the signals that are responsible for sudden mood change. Increasing intake in the diet as well as through

Essential nutrients

Research has found that children with ADHD are lacking in:

- *Essential fatty acids omega-3 and omega-6*

- *B-group vitamins*

- *Chromium*

- *Zinc*

- *Magnesium*

- *Vitamin C*

supplementation has been shown to improve brain metabolism and the symptoms of ADHD.

A lack of thiamine (vitamin B_1) also is linked to aggressive, erratic and impulsive behaviour. Potatoes, whole grains, nuts, seeds, eggs, meat, vegetables and brown rice are good sources of B_1. Vitamin B_6 is equally important.

Numerous studies suggest there is a connection between food allergies or intolerances (see below) and behavioural problems, including ADHD. Some nutrition experts believe that sugar may not be the main factor when it comes to behavioural problems but that an allergy or intolerance to the additives, particularly colourings, often used in sweets and sugary foods, lies at the root of the problem. Eliminating food allergens has proved effective in treating children with ADHD.

ALLERGIES & INTOLERANCES

A food allergy occurs when the immune system overreacts to a normally harmless substance in a food by producing antibodies. It can cause a wide range of symptoms from a runny nose and diarrhoea to a potentially life-threatening reaction such as swelling of the throat suffered by those who are allergic to nuts, for example. Somewhat confusingly, a child can test negatively for an allergy but may still react to certain foods. This is known as a food intolerance, which is often caused by a digestive problem.

Food intolerances are characterised by adverse reactions such as fuzzy headedness, poor concentration, headaches, rashes, asthma,

eczema and behavioural problems that arise over hours or even days.

Allergies and intolerances tend to run in families so if you or your partner suffer from an allergy or intolerance, then the chances are fairly likely that your child will develop one, too. Children are also more susceptible to food intolerance because of their immature digestive and immune systems. Reassuringly, while the number of cases of food intolerance appears to be increasing, the number of people with severe food allergies is still rare. The most common food allergens include dairy products, eggs, tomatoes, citrus fruit, wheat, nuts, soya and shellfish. Always consult your doctor or dietitian about allergy testing and before eliminating any food from your children's diets.

Dairy products are one of the most common causes of food allergies, but there are several non-dairy substitutes available.

BestBUYS

So far, this book has concentrated on the individual nutrients and foods that can benefit your child and the substances that will hold back his or her progress. Now it's time to consider how you shop for food. Buy it wisely and your children will get the maximum nutritional benefits from their food.

Concerns about chemicals in our food mean that many of us are opting for organic produce. Since it's believed that children are more vulnerable to the effects of pesticide residues than adults (see box, page 29), buying organic food for them makes even more sense. You may have to pay slightly more for organic products, but they are generally tastier, fresher and more nutritious.

Farmers' markets are popular and provide a great way of ensuring you buy the freshest, best-quality, locally grown produce.

FRUIT & VEGETABLES

Whenever you shop for fruit and vegetables, you need to buy the freshest you can get. The longer fruit and vegetables are left hanging around, the less nutrients they will contain. Therefore, it's a good idea to shop in stores that have a high turnover. Try to avoid fruit and vegetables that have been displayed outdoors or in a hot, lighted window, since nutrient levels will have diminished. Fluorescent lighting can have the same effect.

Most supermarkets sell a good selection of organic fruit and vegetables. Organic fruit and vegetables tend to taste better because they are not intensively grown and so do not absorb excessive water. Some studies have shown that the lower levels of water in organic fruit and vegetables mean that they contain a higher concentration of vitamins and minerals. Organic produce is generally grown in better quality soil and left to ripen longer on the plant, rather than being artificially ripened, which can affect flavour and nutrient levels.

However, much organic produce is grown abroad and so the time between picking the food and eating it is longer than would occur with locally grown fruit and vegetables. Fortunately, some supermarkets and

Did you know?

IS IT FRESH?

Some fruit and vegetables are older than they look! Apples can be stored for anything up to 12 months in controlled temperature atmosphere. Likewise, carrots can be around for up to nine months, while potatoes can be up to 12 months old if kept in cold storage. Potatoes intended for long-term storage may also be sprayed with a chemical sprout-inhibitor. Apples and oranges are also routinely waxed to give them a sheen and seal in moisture, after which they are hot-air dried. Look for organic, seasonal and preferably local fruit and vegetables. Buy unwaxed fruit if possible. Look for firm, unblemished produce and be slightly suspicious of special offers, since they may indicate that the retailer has a surplus of produce near its sell-by date.

greengrocers are beginning to stock more and more local produce. For fresh local food, try farmers' markets, box schemes or buying direct from the farms themselves – this also is often a cheaper way to buy organic.

Wherever you shop, it's a good idea to buy fruit and vegetables in small quantities on a regular basis. Choose loose produce as it will be much easier to check for quality – and you won't be taking home unwanted packaging. Remember to remove the goods from any plastic bags when storing.

MEAT, FISH & EGGS

Worries about what's been put in meat or fish and where it's come from mean that many families are already choosing organic options. Organic meat and poultry comes from animals that are not routinely fed antibiotics and hormones, and that have been farmed under higher standards of animal welfare and with strict controls on feed. No genetically modified (GM) ingredients are allowed. Because meat is high in saturated fat, purchase leaner cuts such as fillet of beef.

Sausages make a quick convenient lunch or supper but they do vary hugely in quality. Buy the most expensive products you can afford with the highest quantity of meat (at least 85–90 per cent), preferably organic, and with few fillers and additives. The same goes for bacon and the like. There are vegetarian alternatives available, but these can contain an alarming number of unwanted additives.

When buying fish, wild or organically farmed animals are preferable to conventionally farmed fish that may have been given pesticides and additives such as colourings – just look at the difference in colour between farmed and wild salmon. Undyed smoked haddock and cod also are better choices than their bright yellow alternatives.

When shopping for fresh fish and meat, it is easier to check quality and freshness if you buy over-the-counter – whether that's in the supermarket, butchers, fishmongers or at a farmers' market.

When buying eggs, look for organic and free-range. They will come from hens kept in preferable living conditions that are given a natural diet and not routinely fed on antibiotics or yolk-enhancing dyes. Boxes depicting attractive countryside scenes or including the words 'farm fresh' mean little – the eggs are just as likely to come from battery farms. Store eggs in the fridge, where they will keep for a couple of weeks.

PACKAGED OR PREPARED FOODS

If you're buying packaged or prepared foods you need to check the labelling to see what ingredients and additives they contain. You want to avoid those with high amounts of sugar, saturated and hydrogenated (trans) fats, colourings, additives, flavourings, preservatives and artificial sweeteners, many of which have been linked to behavioural problems, hyperactivity and food allergies in children.

Fish fingers, chicken nuggets and beef-burgers are popular with children but are highly processed and likely to contain substantial amounts of fat, salt, colourings and additives. There are no official rules covering such

products, which means that they don't have to include a specified percentage of meat (often they contain less than 40 per cent) and they tend to be made with chopped, reformed or shaped meat.

Choose fish without batter or breadcrumbs, which can be an excuse for manufacturers to add colourings, preservatives, fat and cheap fillers, or if you can't resist the crumbed version, look for the brand with the highest fish content and lowest number of additives and colourings (or make your own home-made breadcrumbs). Bear in mind that when you look at the list on a label, the first ingredient is the one found in the highest quantity.

Pizzas are perfect ready-made meals – take them straight from the fridge or freezer and they cook in a matter of minutes – but they are

often seen as junk food. Of course many of the pizzas on sale are, but it is increasingly easy to find decent quality pizzas made with natural ingredients. Delis often sell delicious homemade pizza by the slice and of course you can make your own, see page 61.

STORE-CUPBOARD, FRIDGE AND FREEZER FOODS

When you've got hungry mouths to feed, you don't want to be popping out to the shops before every meal, so make sure your cupboards, fridge and freezer are kept well stocked. Below we set out the best stand-bys to have on hand so you can plan meals that are healthy and nutritious for your children.

Cereal staples

Pasta must be one of the ultimate convenience foods – easy to cook and the perfect base for so many meals. It's also very popular with most children. There is a huge range of different shapes to try, as well as coloured pastas – just make sure you buy the sort with natural colouring (such as spinach and tomato). Dried pasta keeps well stored in an airtight container and you can keep fresh pasta in the freezer.

Rice and noodles also are ideal starting points for many dishes and you might find it useful to have more than one kind of rice in stock. Keep a long-grain or easy-cook rice (preferably brown) to make pilafs or to serve with curries and stir-fries, some arborio or carnaroli rice for making risottos, and a pudding rice for some good old-fashioned milk puddings. And don't forget couscous and buckwheat – so easy to cook and turn into

delicious meals with just a few flavourings. Add a spoonful of pesto, some chopped herbs or some raisins and toasted nuts. Or make a warm salad of grains by stirring in some chopped tomato, cucumber and feta cheese.

Breakfast cereals are a vital item in any family's store-cupboard. They're a convenient way to give your children a healthy start in the morning – if you choose wisely. Avoid sugar-rich cereals and opt for sugar-free or low-sugar, whole-grain cereals.

Canned and packaged foods

Some canned vegetables can be a useful alternative to fresh or frozen vegetables. Children often love sweetcorn and the canned sort is convenient and readily available. Look for the no-added-sugar and no-added-salt versions and rinse well before using. Canned lentils and beans, already soaked and cooked, cut down cooking time by hours.

Baked beans are a popular quick meal for children and adults alike so a few tins of organic baked beans are a useful stand-by. Look for brands that are lower in salt and sugar but try to avoid artificial sweeteners added in place of sugar. Half a tin of baked beans counts as one of the recommended five daily portions of fruit and vegetables.

A variety of fish comes canned, such as sardines, mackerel, salmon and tuna, all of which can be turned into tasty meals or sandwich fillings. They're also a good source of those omega-3 fatty acids, albeit in lower amounts than found in fresh fish.

Canned soup can be high in salt and sugar and it's relatively quick to make your own. If

in many different forms and you can get a version that's lower in salt and sugar, and made with organic ingredients.

High-fruit, no-added-sugar jams and spreads have an intensively fruity flavour and a higher ratio of fruit to sugar than cheaper alternatives. They may be slightly more expensive but they are worth it in terms of fruit content and flavour. You will need to keep them in the fridge as they won't keep in the same way as traditional jams.

Nut butters such as peanut, cashew or hazelnut provide an energy-dense snack if spread on bread, crumpets or muffins. Look for those brands that have the fewest additives and no added sugar. Unsalted nuts and seeds also make convenient snacks but don't give children under five whole nuts and avoid them altogether if there is any history of nut allergy in your family. Try toasting nuts and seeds to add to their flavour. Nuts quickly become rancid once shelled, so buy them in the shells and store in an airtight container until needed.

Dried fruit is an energy-packed source of vitamins and minerals, including iron. The choice is extensive but look for unsulphured fruit. Sulphur dioxide is used as a preservative and can provoke asthma attacks in susceptible children. Dried fruit is a valuable ingredient in many dishes, both sweet and savoury and the small packs of dried fruit are perfect for lunch boxes or snacks.

Breadsticks, rice, oat or corn cakes make ideal snacks and are healthier alternatives to

you use stock cubes or powder (often known as bouillon powder), avoid those that are high in salt and contain artificial colourings and flavourings. Keep a few sachets of miso soup in the cupboard. Just add hot water to the powdered miso and then pour over noodles and steamed vegetables. Sprinkle with some sesame seeds for a quick, healthy meal.

Treats and snacks

You can't keep kids away from some of those little treats that make meal times more fun for them. You can, however, find healthier versions of some of their favourites. Tomato ketchup, for example, now comes

salty and fatty crisps and similar snacks. Try to avoid those that contain artificial additives such as the flavour enhancer monosodium glutamate – the fewer the ingredients the better.

You also can buy a range of fruit bars, low-sugar cereal bars or natural fruit chewy sweets that are useful to keep for snacks and lunch boxes. These are preferable to the high-sugar, high-colour, high-additive, gelatine-filled alternatives generally available.

And last, but not least, keep everyone happy with some good-quality chocolate. A popular treat with all the family as well as a vital cooking ingredient, chocolate needs to have at least 30 per cent cocoa solids for milk and 55 per cent for plain. Avoid bars with unwanted additives and if buying white chocolate, choose bars made with pure cocoa butter and not vegetable fat.

REFRIGERATED FOODS

When you're rustling up a meal – whether it's a quick tea or a Sunday lunch – the fridge is usually your first port of call. Where would we be without eggs, milk and cheese – all of which keep best when chilled? Eggs are ideal for a light meal as well as being an essential ingredient in many recipes. Butter and non-hydrogenated spreads are preferable to margarines and spreads containing trans or hydrogenated fats and other additives, which are just as bad for our health as saturated fat.

Cheese is a perfect stand-by ingredient – use it to top pizzas or make a macaroni cheese, or keep some for snacks. Avoid heavily processed cheeses, so often aimed at children, and buy good quality, preferably organic, cheese.

Small-sized portions of items like ham and cheese aimed at children's lunch boxes are easy to find. However, these are usually high in artificial additives and are best avoided. Instead, buy good-quality ham, pâté or cheese when you want something to pop in your child's lunch box.

A tub of humous is a great snack and lunch stand-by. Give it to children with strips of pitta bread or carrot sticks for a healthy dip, or put it in their sandwiches. You even can stir it into soups and stews for added flavour. Use pesto in the same way or stir it into pasta, rice or even mashed potato for a real change.

It's always a good idea to have some yogurt in the fridge for a quick and easy dessert. However, some brands contain little fruit and are often laden with added colours, flavours, sugar, artificial sweeteners and gelatine. Go for

BIO YOGURTS

Most of us are familiar with the bio yogurts now available, but why do we need them? A healthy gut is very important and ensures that foods are digested well and nutrients are transported to where they are needed. The healthy bacteria in bio yogurts may help the immune system to resist tummy bugs and, if eaten after a course of antibiotics, may restore the internal flora of the intestines – which is particularly important for children.

those that contain real fruit. If you keep a large pot of plain yogurt or fromage frais in the fridge you can flavour it yourself. Try chopped banana, home-made fresh fruit purées, toasted nuts and seeds or a spoonful of maple syrup.

Tofu (also known as soya bean curd) is a useful stand-by, especially if anyone in your family is vegetarian. Rich in calcium and a good source of protein, it can be very versatile. Try it roasted or stir fried, after marinating in black bean sauce or a mixture of garlic, ginger, honey and sesame oil.

Soup makes a wonderful quick meal but canned and packet soups are best avoided since they tend to be high in sugar and salt. If you want to buy ready-made soup, then go for the 'fresh' soups from the chiller section and store them in the freezer.

Frozen vegetables can contain higher amounts of nutrients, such as vitamin C and iron, than fresh produce since they are often

frozen very soon after picking, whereas fresh vegetables may be around for quite a while before they land on our plates. Therefore, a few packs of frozen vegetables make a valuable addition to any freezer. Broccoli, broad beans, spinach, sweetcorn or carrots are all useful stand-bys as are, of course, peas – sometimes the only vegetable that some kids will eat!

DRINKS

There are now so many different types of fruit juice around that choosing the most natural and healthiest can be tricky. The best way to get beneficial amounts of vitamins without additives is to make fruit juice at home from good quality, organic fresh fruit. If you have a juicer and a freezer then you can make some in batches and freeze to store.

In the shops, you'll find chilled, ready-made, freshly squeezed juices or smoothies and these contain useful amounts of vitamins, although some are destroyed during the manufacturing process. Be aware that bottles and cartons labelled as fruit drinks can contain as little as five per cent fruit juice, along with added sugar or artificial sweeteners and additives. Remarkably, some fruit-flavoured drinks contain no real fruit at all. They may have added vitamins but this does not make them healthy drinks. And watch out for those drinks sold in the chiller cabinet that are masquerading as real fruit juice – they're not all that they seem!

Bear in mind that all fruit juices and drinks contain sugar, whether it is natural or not, so can cause tooth decay. Dilute juice with water or only serve at meal times and get children to brush their teeth regularly.

Cooking SMART

The way you cook and prepare food influences its nutritional content. Certain cooking methods will preserve nutrients, cut out excess fat and protect against disease-causing organisms. Make sure any frozen products are thoroughly defrosted before cooking.

VEGETABLES

Generally speaking, eating raw fruit and vegetables will be most beneficial. Make sure you wash vegetables before using, but do not soak them because water-soluble nutrients will leach into the water. Hold root vegetables such as carrots under cold running water and use a vegetable scrubbing brush to remove dirt.

Many nutrients are found in or just below the skin so avoid peeling them, if at all possible. If your children like their vegetables peeled, you can cook them in their skins first and then peel them.

When you're making a meal, it's best not to prepare vegetables too far in advance of cooking or serving, as nutrients, such as vitamin C, will diminish as soon as the cut surface is exposed to air. The same is true of fruit. Once cooked, serve vegetables as soon as possible because they will begin to lose their nutritional content if they stand.

Steaming or stir-frying is preferable to boiling – the latter destroys water-soluble vitamins such as B and C. Cooking vegetables whole or in large pieces helps to preserve their nutritional content. Keep the cooking water and use it as a stock.

MEAT

As well as choosing leaner cuts, you also should trim off all extra visible fat. This will reduce the cooking time by about 20 per cent. Fat-free cooking methods such as stewing, braising or grilling are best. If you are making a casserole, you should skim off the fat at regular intervals. If you are going to fry meat, which is best avoided, make sure you use olive or rapeseed oils in place of butter. Both these oils are high in monounsaturated fats. Alternatively, use a non-stick frying pan. Place roasting meats on a rack to allow fat to drip off while cooking.

POULTRY

Rinse the poultry thoroughly, including the cavity if you are cooking a whole bird. If roasting a whole bird, prick the skin to allow the fat to run out, and place on a rack. Make sure poultry is cooked thoroughly to protect against any possibility of salmonella poisoning. If using a thermometer, it should read 82°C for a whole bird (in the thickest part) and 77°C for pieces. Alternatively, pierce the poultry with a fork and make sure the juices run clear. Stir-frying, poaching and baking are low-fat cooking methods. Always remove the skin before serving as this contains high levels of fat.

Meal TIMES

For mental clarity, sustained energy levels and concentration, it's not just what children eat that matters but when. Children are particularly vulnerable to dips in blood-sugar levels that can lead to mood swings, irritability and poor attention. Regular healthy meals, supplemented by nutritious snacks and sufficient fluids are crucial throughout the day to maintain steady blood-sugar levels.

BREAKFAST

It is now widely recognised by nutrition experts, and supported by research, that children who eat a decent breakfast perform better at school. Breakfast is seen as the most important meal of the day since it replenishes vital brain nutrients and blood-sugar (glucose) levels that are depleted overnight. Breakfast also kick-starts the metabolism, which slows down overnight. Moreover, research has shown that skipping the first meal of the day can lead to children developing an unhealthy pattern of snacking on high-fat, high-sugar foods. This is particularly true of children who leave the house on empty

Breakfast ideas

Nutritionists say that the perfect breakfast should satisfy the appetite and provide long-term energy without being too high in fat or giving an immediate sugar rush – which is what would happen if you gave children a sugar-laden breakfast cereal. It should provide 25 per cent of a child's daily nutrient requirement. Turn to page 49 for breakfast recipes but other quick suggestions to start the day include:

- *Porridge with sliced banana*

- *Boiled or poached egg on wholemeal toast*

- *Low-sugar breakfast cereal with fruit and milk*

- *Fresh fruit smoothie*

- *Yogurt with fruit*

- *Beans on wholemeal toast*

- *Grilled tomato and bacon or sausages with wholemeal toast*

- *Pancakes made with wholemeal flour, topped with fruit*

- *Wholemeal muffin or bread with low-sugar jam, yeast extract or peanut butter*

- *Poached or grilled fish*

stomachs and stop to buy sweets and crisps on the way to school.

Many studies show that, compared to children who do eat breakfast, those who skip this meal do not perform as well in areas such as numeracy, problem solving, information selection and recall, and language skills. This is because the body needs fuel on waking and when it doesn't get the sustenance it needs, it switches to survival mode and only releases energy for emergencies. This means that the body and, more specifically, the brain are without the glucose they so badly need. Symptoms such as lack of concentration and poor memory are all indications that the brain is struggling due to low levels of fuel.

CARBOHYDRATES OR PROTEIN?

In the main, it is believed that the positive influence of breakfast on brain function is because the meal is usually based on carbohydrates – breakfast cereals and toast are good examples. Cereals are often fortified with vitamins and minerals, including the B vitamins and iron, which help with energy production. They also provide glucose, which is the main fuel for the brain, while the milk poured over cereals is a good source of calcium, B-group vitamins, zinc and magnesium.

Controversially, there is also research to suggest that a protein-based breakfast is more successful in stimulating the brain and satisfies the appetite quicker and for longer than a carbohydrate meal. It's believed that this is because the protein meal encourages the release of chemicals that increase alertness and boost reaction times. This means that protein foods such as eggs, milk, yogurt, beans and fish may play a greater role in getting the brain fired up in the morning. The best policy, since the ratio of protein to carbohydrate is unknown, is to make sure you include both in each meal, and that includes breakfast.

LUNCH

A wholesome lunch, whether it be home-cooked, packed or a school lunch, is vital for maintaining energy levels and sustaining memory, concentration and learning for the rest

nutrient
KNOW-HOW

QUICK SNACK IDEAS

- Wholemeal muffin with mashed banana
- Oatcakes with cream cheese
- Eggy bread
- Boiled egg with toast fingers, spread with yeast extract
- Peanut butter on sesame-seed bagel
- Humous and vegetable sticks
- Dried fruit and nuts
- Roasted sunflower and pumpkin seeds
- Crumpet
- Fruit sticks: slices of apple, melon, peach
- Handful of grapes or strawberries
- Toasted teacakes

of the day. School meals have been the target of criticism for some time, and many local authorities have addressed these concerns by ensuring there are healthy options among the chips, fish fingers and beans. Unfortunately, where children are able to select their own lunches, these healthier alternatives are often ignored. What's more, children are usually unfamiliar with the rules of a balanced diet and tend to overload their plates with the high-refined carbohydrate, high-fat options.

If you're able to send your child to school with a packed lunch this is often good way of monitoring his or her diet. When time is short, it can be tricky to be inspired about packed lunches and it's very easy to get stuck in the 'sandwich, crisps, chocolate bar and an apple' rut. Variety is the key, try offering different types of fruit, half an avocado, a kiwi fruit, cubes of melon or dried fruit, for example. There are plenty of different kinds of bread to choose from such as tortilla, mini rolls, bagels, ciabatta or muffins. A flask is perfect for holding soup for a warming winter lunch or try rice, potato or pasta salads. See pages 44–5 for more tips and ideas for lunch boxes.

Following on from the controversial research that suggests breakfast should include a higher ratio of protein food to carbohydrate, some nutritionists believe that lunch should adopt similar guidelines. Protein foods are believed to be better for mental stimulation and alertness and will help to avoid the mid-afternoon dip in energy that many children experience. On the other hand, the general rule is that carbohydrate foods, which are converted into glucose, are the brain's most important source of fuel and should play a major part in every meal throughout the day.

SNACKS

In the past, dietitians have discouraged eating between meals but there is mounting evidence to suggest that kids need to eat little and often, since stores of glucose are used up more quickly in children than in adults. In fact it's good for children to have a couple of snacks – albeit healthy ones – during the day to maintain brain efficiency by keeping blood-sugar levels steady. Avoid the short-term boost given by high-fat, high-sugar snacks and drinks. The sugar-high is followed by a sugar-slump, often resulting in mood swings and irritability. It also may be beneficial to provide a carbohydrate-based snack such as toast, a muffin or a crumpet, an hour or two before bedtime since carbohydrates are said to encourage the production of the calming brain chemical serotonin. A snack also will keep hunger at bay during the night since dips in blood-sugar levels may be a reason for a child waking in the night.

DINNER

Originating from the same study that suggested we should eat more protein at breakfast and lunch is the finding that dinner should include a higher proportion of carbohydrate to protein. Carbohydrates, such as pasta, rice, couscous and potatoes, trigger the release of the brain chemical serotonin, which is said to induce feelings of calm and encourage sleep (see page 23). If your child is particularly active or hyper at the end of the day it could be well worth increasing the amount of carbohydrates he or she eats at this time. However, don't forget the importance of protein, too. It's vital to eat a variety of protein foods to get a balance of the essential amino acids that have to be provided by diet and that are necessary for building the brain's messengers. Opt for good-quality organic meat, fish, eggs, beans, lentils, cheese, nuts and seeds. For many children, this is the main meal of the day and it can be an opportunity to encourage your child to top up their intake of fruit and vegetables to reach the recommended daily intake of five portions.

LUNCH BOXES

Though many parents dread the daily grind of coming up with something edible to put into the lunch box, with a little advance planning, a packed lunch can make a major contribution to an all-round healthy diet.

THE TRIMMINGS

It may sound odd to pay attention to the box itself, before discussing what goes in it, but appearances are more important to children than most adults care to acknowledge. You are more likely to receive a favourable uptake on your packed lunch if you provide an attractive container and appropriate cutlery and napkin, where necessary. Choose a rigid lunch box to protect the contents and only buy a box with a decorative theme if it is age appropriate and your child approves. Some boxes contain freezer pads to help keep food cool which is a good idea, especially in summer. Boxes also come divided into compartments, which seems a useful idea until you try to force food into each slot. A flask can be useful for keeping soups warm and drinks cool depending on the season.

AVERAGE CHOICE

It's incredibly easy to be misled by food industry claims when short on time and inspiration. This box's contents may have promised much but delivers little.

Concentrated fruit drinks corrode tooth enamel and are low in fruit content.

Bananas are a perfect source of energy but are lunch box nightmares – if they aren't squashed they turn black and ooze over other food.

Many manufactured cereal bars contain little 'slow release' energy. They are high in sugar and calories, and expensive.

White bread has had fibre and nutrients removed. Its filling, 'processed meat paste', is heavy on additives to provide flavour and contains the cheapest cuts of meat.

Cartons of fruit dessert contain little fruit, lots of refined sugar and are not filling.

Potato crisps are high in fat and many additives. If you opt for low-fat, be aware that it is usually replaced by sugar or chemical binding agents.

BEST CHOICE

The contents of the lunch box below reflect how you should think about nutritional content. You need to include both protein and carbohydrate foods to provide energy throughout the day and to aid concentration, memory, IQ and attention span. Fresh fruit and vegetables are also a must.

Vary the contents as much as possible, and if you know your child dislikes a food, resist the temptation to keep slipping it in in the hope he will eat it, however good it may be for him.

- Yogurt or fromage frais in tubes act as cooler sticks if pre-frozen. Only buy those with a high real fruit content. Alternatively, make your own flavoured variety – stir a fruit purée or coulis into a pot of natural live bio yoghurt.

- Vitamin C-rich fruit will encourage iron absorption and aid energy production.

- Diluted fresh fruit juice or water are preferable to concentrates or carbonated drinks in terms of tooth decay and calories; energy should always be provided by slow-release foods rather than liquids. Good hydration is essential to maintain concentration.

- Spears of celery and carrot as well as red pepper, cucumber, mangetout, etc., provide a range of vitamins and can be dipped into humous.

- By making your own cereal bars (see page 50) you can control the ingredients used and save money.

- Wholemeal bread provides extra roughage and is more nutritious than white. Butter can quickly become 'sweaty' so try a thin spread of mayonnaise to provide a creamy taste or add extra lettuce to prevent fillings tasting dry. Cheese, egg, canned fish or good quality ham are quick and healthy options and provide a protein boost.

Brainboosting
RECIPES

These recipes are created with children in mind, but will also be enjoyed by adults, in an effort to make all family meals easier to prepare and more fun to enjoy. They contain the foods that are said to be most beneficial for the brain and those that have been shown, in some instances, to improve IQ, memory, attention span and concentration.

A GOOD START

The most important meal of the day, breakfast replenishes vital brain nutrients and energy depleted overnight. Recent research suggests that children who eat a decent breakfast perform better at school.

FRUIT & NUT CLEVER CLUSTERS

Most breakfast cereals contain excessive amounts of sugar and perhaps surprisingly salt – a bowl of cornflakes can contain more sodium than a packet of crisps! Try making this crunchy cereal – it's a type of granola that's a nutritious mixture of fruits, nuts, oats and seeds, providing plenty of sustained energy for the day ahead. You can easily adapt this recipe to include favourite dried fruits.

About 20 portions
100g/¾ cup whole hazelnuts
60g/scant ½ cup blanched almonds
250g/2½ cups whole porridge oats
70g/½ cup sunflower seeds
35g/¼ cup sesame seeds
3 tbsp omega-blend oil or sunflower oil
6 tbsp honey
100g/¾ cup chopped dried dates
100g/¾ cup ready-to-eat unsulphured
   dried apricots, roughly chopped
milk or live natural bio yogurt, to serve

1 Preheat the oven to 140°C/275°F. Place the hazelnuts and almonds in a plastic bag and crush with a rolling pin until roughly broken. Place the crushed nuts in a bowl with the oats and seeds.
2 Heat the oil and honey gently in a saucepan until the honey has just melted. Stir the mixture into the oats, nuts and seeds.
3 Spread the mixture in an even layer on two baking sheets and bake for

35 minutes, stirring occasionally, until golden and slightly crisp (the mixture will become more crispy as it cools).
4 Transfer the mixture to a bowl and mix in the dates and apricots, then leave to cool. Store in an airtight jar until ready to eat. Serve with milk or live natural bio yogurt.

Nuts and seeds contain plenty of brain-boosting nutrients, being an excellent source of B-group vitamins, iron, vitamin E, zinc, selenium and omega-6 essential fatty acids. **Whole oats** are a complex carbohydrate, which help to keep blood-sugar levels steady, enabling the brain to work more efficiently.

WONDER CRUNCH

A muesli-type cereal featuring a brain-nurturing combination of whole grains, nuts, seeds and fruit, hence the name 'wonder'.

About 20 portions
75g/¾ cup flaked almonds
60g/½ cup chopped Brazil nuts
70g/½ cup sunflower seeds
55g/scant ½ cup pumpkin seeds
400g/4 cups wheat flakes
200g/1½ cups unsulphured dried
   apricots, finely chopped
200g/1¼ cups raisins

1 Lightly toast the almonds, Brazil nuts, sunflower and pumpkin seeds in a dry frying pan over a medium heat for 3 minutes, stirring frequently, until golden. Leave to cool.
2 Combine the toasted nuts and seeds, wheat flakes and dried fruit in a large bowl, mix well. Transfer to an airtight container and store until ready to eat. Serve with milk, live natural bio yogurt and fresh fruit, if liked.

Wheat flakes provide a rich array of nutrients and although mainly a complex carbohydrate food, they also contain a certain amount of protein, both of which are essential fuel for the brain and keep energy and blood-sugar levels steady.

POWER BREAKFAST BARS

Breakfast is undoubtedly the most important meal of the day, replenishing the brain after a night's sleep. Yet when time is short – especially on school days – this oat, apple and seed cereal bar can be a real boon. Serve with a glass of milk or fresh fruit juice.

Makes 10 slices

100g/1 stick unsalted butter
100g/generous ½ cup light muscovado sugar
4 tbsp golden syrup or honey
250g/2½ cups rolled porridge oats
2 tbsp sunflower seeds
1 tbsp sesame seeds
1 tbsp pumpkin seeds
1 dessert apple, cored and grated

1 Preheat the oven to 180°C/350°F. Grease and base-line a 20 cm/8 in square cake tin. Melt the butter in a saucepan over a low heat and add the sugar and syrup or honey. Heat until just warm – do not allow to boil.
2 Put the porridge oats, seeds and apple in a mixing bowl and pour on the buttery syrup. Mix well until combined and spoon the mixture into the prepared tin.
3 Bake for 25–30 minutes until golden and slightly crisp. Cut into 10 bars while still warm and leave in the tin until cool and crisp.

BANANA YOGURT

This simple breakfast provides plenty of brain-sustaining protein as well as essential vitamins and minerals for the day ahead. Live natural bio yogurt contains beneficial bacteria which restores equilibrium in the gut, especially following a course of antibiotics or a stomach upset. It also helps to increase the uptake of nutrients.

Serves 2

2 tbsp mixed seeds such as sunflower, pumpkin and sesame
2 small bananas
230g/1 cup live natural bio yogurt
2 tsp maple syrup

1 Lightly toast the seeds in a dry frying pan until just golden, tossing frequently.
2 Slice the bananas into two glasses or bowls. Top with the yogurt, then sprinkle with the seeds. Drizzle each serving with the maple syrup.

BRAIN BOX

Despite their size, **seeds** are a powerhouse of brain nutrients, particularly omega-6 essential fatty acids (pumpkin seeds also provide omega-3), zinc, magnesium and vitamin E.

APPLE CROISSANT

The lightly spiced apple compote makes a delicious filling for a warmed croissant. It also can be puréed and stirred into a live bio yogurt for a healthy change to shop-bought yogurts.

Serves 2
2 dessert apples, cored, peeled and roughly diced
½ tsp ground cinnamon
small knob of butter
squeeze fresh lemon juice
6 tbsp water
2 croissants
sprinkling toasted almonds
live natural bio yogurt, to serve

BRAIN BOX

Yogurt is a top-class protein food and a great way to kick-start the body and motivate the brain first-thing in the morning.

1 Put the apples, cinnamon, butter, lemon juice (this prevents the apple browning) and water in a heavy-based, non-metallic saucepan. Simmer, half-covered, over a medium heat for 20 minutes, until the apples are tender. Lightly mash the apples with a fork to break them down slightly.
2 Warm the croissants, split in half and spoon the apples into the centres. Sprinkle with toasted almonds and serve with a spoonful of live natural bio yogurt.

VERY MERRY BERRY YOGURT

Many children dislike 'bits' in their food which unfortunately can put them off berries. This compote is sieved to remove any offending seeds and skin, resulting in an intensely fruity and tasty red sauce. It is delicious stirred into a live natural bio yogurt with a sprinkling of granola.

Serves 2–4
300g/2 cups mixed berries such as strawberries or raspberries
1–2 tbsp caster sugar, to taste
1 tbsp cornflour
Fruit & Nut Clever Clusters (see page 49), to serve
live natural bio yogurt, to serve

1 Rinse then hull the fruit. Purée the mixed berries in a food processor or

BRAIN BOX

Berries contain powerful antioxidants known as anthocyanidins, which have been found to protect the brain from the damaging effects of free radicals and toxins.

blender. Sieve the purée into a pan to remove any skin and seeds. Add a little sugar and the cornflour to the pan and heat gently and briefly, stirring frequently, until thickened. Taste and add a little more sugar, if necessary.
2 Place a few spoonfuls of the Fruit & Nut Clever Clusters in a glass or bowl, top with a few spoonfuls of yogurt, then some of the berry purée. Top with more yogurt and a final sprinkling of Fruit & Nut Clusters.

PORRIDGE WITH APRICOT SPLODGE

A bowl of warming porridge makes the perfect start to the day. Oats are digested slowly in the body, helping to maintain energy levels by keeping blood-sugar levels steady. Sprinkle with a few linseeds before serving, if liked.

Serves 2
100g/1 cup porridge oats
1 tsp wheatgerm (optional)
250ml/1 cup milk
2 tsp clear honey, to serve (optional)
a sprinkling of linseeds, to serve (optional)

for the apricot splodge:
125g/1 cup ready-to-eat unsulphured apricots, roughly chopped
150ml/²⁄₃ cup fresh apple juice (not concentrated)
150ml/²⁄₃ cup water

1 To make the apricot splodge, place the apricots in a saucepan with the apple juice and water. Bring to the boil, cover, then reduce the heat and simmer for 30 minutes or until the apricots are tender. Place the apricots and any liquid left in the pan, in a blender or food processor and purée until smooth. Set aside to cool.
2 To make the porridge, put the oats and wheatgerm, if using, into a saucepan with the milk. Bring to the boil, stirring occasionally. Reduce the heat and simmer, stirring frequently, for 4 minutes until smooth and creamy.
3 Spoon the porridge into two bowls, top with a spoonful of apricot splodge or mix the purée in to give a swirly effect. Top with a spoonful of honey and a sprinkling of linseeds, if liked.

DATE & VANILLA ENERGY SPREAD

This makes a healthier, low-sugar alternative to commercially made jams, which by their nature are high in sugar and, with the cheaper brands, low in fruit. A spoonful of this rich spread is delicious on a wholemeal muffin, brioche or toasted crumpet. It can also be served with yogurt, porridge or as a filling in pancakes.

200g/1½ cups chopped dried dates
250ml/1 cup water
1 tsp vanilla extract

1 Place the dates and water in a heavy-based saucepan. Bring to the boil, then reduce the heat and simmer, covered, for 20 minutes until the fruit is tender and most of the water has been absorbed.
2 Transfer to a food processor or blender and add the vanilla extract; purée until smooth. Set aside to cool and store in an airtight container in the fridge, where the spread will keep for up to a week.

EYE-SPY EGGS

This nifty breakfast catches the imagination of children and is perfect brain fuel for the day ahead, being a nutritious combination of protein and carbohydrates. Grilled tomatoes or baked beans add the finishing touch!

Serves 1
1 slice seedy wholemeal bread
butter, for spreading
1 egg
grilled tomatoes or baked beans, to
    serve

1 Preheat the grill to high. Stamp out a circle, about 5 cm (2 in) in diameter, in the centre of the slice of bread using a pastry cutter.
2 Line the grill pan with foil. Toast one side of the bread. Turn the bread over, spread the top with butter and break the egg into the hole in the centre. Grill for 3–5 minutes until just set.
3 Using a fish slice, carefully lift the toast and egg together and transfer to a serving plate. Serve immediately with grilled tomatoes or baked beans.

POTATO CAKES WITH BACON

A great way of using up leftover mashed potato, these savoury mini potato pancakes are equally good served with grilled tomatoes, good quality sausages or baked beans or drizzled with maple syrup, if liked.

Serves 4
100g/scant ½ cup cold mashed potato
200ml/scant 1 cup milk
75g/⅓ cup wholemeal self-raising flour
pinch of salt
1 egg, beaten
sunflower oil, for frying
good-quality bacon, grilled until crisp,
    to serve
grilled tomatoes, to serve (optional)
maple syrup, to serve (optional)

1 Blend the mashed potato and milk in a food processor or blender to make a thin potato purée.
2 Put the flour and salt in a bowl, make a well in the centre of the flour and add the beaten egg, then gradually add the potato purée. Whisk to make a smooth, fairly thick batter.
3 Heat a little oil in a large non-stick frying pan. Place a small ladleful of batter per cake into the pan – you will probably need to work in batches. Cook each cake for 2 minutes on each side until golden. Keep the cooked potato cakes warm as you cook.
4 Divide the cakes between the four plates, add a rasher of bacon and grilled tomatoes, or drizzle with maple syrup if using.

BUBBLE & SQUEAK CAKES

Cabbage is not always a favourite with children but usually this has something to do with the soggy veg served up at school. Here, the cabbage is crisp and partly disguised by the cheesy mash. Serve with low-sugar and low-salt baked beans.

Makes 6 patties
60g/½ cup Savoy cabbage, very finely shredded
250g/1 heaping cup cold mashed potato
60g/½ cup mature Cheddar, grated
1 tsp Dijon mustard
salt and pepper, to taste
1 small egg, beaten
flour, for coating
sunflower oil, for frying

1 Steam the cabbage for 3 minutes until just tender. Leave to cool and squeeze with your hands to remove as much water as possible.
2 Mix the cabbage with the mashed potato, cheese and mustard, then season to taste. Stir in the egg and mix until combined.
3 Divide the mixture into six and form each portion into a flat cake using floured hands. Coat each cake in flour and remove any excess.
4 Heat enough oil to lightly coat the bottom of a large heavy-based frying pan with oil. Cook three cakes at a time for 3–4 minutes each side until golden. Drain on kitchen towels before serving.

BRAIN BOX

Cabbage is a valuable source of antioxidant vitamins C, E and beta-carotene, which have a protective effect on the brain. The **cheese** and **egg** both provide valuable brain-boosting protein.

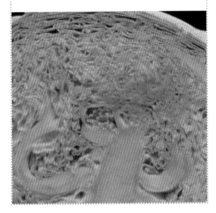

KICK-START BRUNCH

Kids love this complete breakfast in a pan, which is rather similar to an Italian frittata. Chopped bacon, onions or mushrooms can be used instead of the sausage and tomatoes. This dish also makes a perfect after-school tea.

Serves 3–4
3 good quality sausages (or vegetarian alternatives)
sunflower oil, for frying
4 cooked medium-sized potatoes, cooled and cut into quarters
6 cherry tomatoes
salt and pepper, to taste
3 eggs, beaten
wholemeal bread, toasted, to serve

1 Preheat the grill to medium-high. Grill the sausages on a foil-lined grill pan until cooked through and golden brown. Leave to cool slightly, then slice into large chunks.
2 Meanwhile, heat a little oil in a medium-sized heavy-based frying pan with an ovenproof handle. Fry the potatoes until lightly golden all over, then add the tomatoes and cook for a further 2 minutes. Arrange the sausages in the pan so there is an even distribution of potatoes, tomatoes and sausages.
3 Add a little more oil to the pan if it seems dry. Season the beaten eggs and pour the mixture over the ingredients in the pan. Cook for 3 minutes without stirring or disturbing the omelette. Place under the preheated grill for an additional 3 minutes until the top is just cooked. Serve cut into wedges with wholemeal toast.

BRAIN BOX

Salmon is one in a group of oily fish that supply beneficial omega-3 fatty acids, essential for the production of brain cells and improved learning and alertness.

SMOKED SALMON OMELETTE

This may sound a bit 'glam' for a children's book but it works incredibly well and smoked salmon – or smoked trout – can be a useful way to introduce oily fish for children. Served with seedy wholemeal bread, it makes a quick weekend brunch that should be popular with all the family.

Serves 1–2
small knob of butter
2 eggs, beaten
few strips of smoked salmon or trout
freshly ground black pepper, to serve (optional)

1 Melt the butter in a heavy-based, non-stick frying pan and swirl it around to coat the bottom.
2 Pour in the beaten eggs. As the omelette begins to set, push the edges towards the centre, allowing the raw egg to run into the edges of the pan. Cook for about 1 minute and when lightly set and still runny on top, arrange the smoked salmon strips on one half of the omelette. Fold the omelette in half to encase the salmon and cook briefly.
3 Turn out on to a plate and serve, seasoned with freshly ground black pepper, if liked.

QUICK SNACKS

These tasty snacks are useful at any time of day – and the great news is that they are full of goodness, too! Children need to recharge their energy levels more often than adults, so it's a good idea to have some of these readily available.

Zinc has been directly linked to childhood intelligence and its deficiency is disturbingly common. **Beans** are a good source of this valuable mineral, while **tomatoes** are a good source of antioxidant nutrients, lycopene and vitamin C and betacarotene, which protect the brain and nervous system.

TOMATO & BEAN DIP-TASTIC

Spread on oatcakes, wholemeal bread or muffins, this creamy dip makes a nutritious snack.

About 10 servings
3 vine-ripened tomatoes, quartered and seeded
3 garlic cloves, left whole in their skin
2 tbsp omega-blend or extra-virgin olive oil

200g/7oz can cannellini beans, drained and rinsed
2 tbsp fresh lemon juice
salt and pepper, to taste

1 Preheat the oven to 200°C/400°F. Place the tomatoes and garlic in a roasting pan and coat with 1 tbsp oil. Roast for 15 minutes until the garlic is soft and the tomatoes tender.
2 Peel the garlic and tomatoes and place in a food processor or blender with the remaining oil, the beans and lemon juice. Purée until smooth and season to taste. Store in the refrigerator in an airtight container (keeps for up to a week).

AVOCADO DIP

Crunchy raw vegetables seem to be more acceptable to many children than the cooked alternative and dipping them into this nutritious garlicky guacamole adds to the appeal.

Serves 2–4
1 ripe medium avocado
1 small garlic clove, crushed
1 tbsp lemon juice
1 tbsp mayonnaise
various vegetables, to serve, such as broccoli, peppers, celery, baby corn

1 Cut the avocado in half and remove the stone. Scoop the flesh out of the skin. Transfer the flesh to a blender or

processor and add the garlic, lemon juice and mayonnaise. Process until the dip is the consistency you prefer. Alternatively, place the ingredients in a bowl and mash together.
2 Prepare the vegetables to dip into the avocado mixture: cut broccoli and cauliflower into florets; seed peppers and cut into strips; cut celery, cucumber and carrots into sticks, and leave mangetout and baby corn whole. You may wish to blanche the mangetout or corn slightly first. Serve with the dip.

Although **avocados** are fairly high in fat it is the beneficial mono-unsaturated type. Avocados are best eaten when just ripe to get the full benefit of their antioxidant vitamins A, C and E, which protect brain cells against destructive free radicals. They also contain B-group vitamins for memory and clarity of thought.

NUT & SEED SNACK

Crisps contain high amounts of the wrong type of fat, namely saturated, as well as salt and unwanted additives. This soy-flavoured, mixed nut and seed snack makes a nutritious alternative. However, go easy on the soy sauce as it is very salty – only a little is needed to add flavour.

Serves 2
150g/1 cup mixed unsalted raw nuts
   and seeds, such as cashews,
   almonds, hazelnuts, peanuts,
   sunflower and pumpkin seeds
1 tsp soy sauce

WARNING

Children under five should not be given whole nuts because of the danger of choking. If there is a history of peanut allergies in the family or you are concerned about allergies, consult your doctor before giving nuts to children.

1 Preheat the oven to 110°C/225°F. Rub any papery brown skins off the peanuts, if using. Place all the nuts on a baking sheet and roast for 10 minutes, until just golden.
2 Add the seeds and mix well into the nuts. Cook for a further 5 minutes until slightly golden. Pour the soy sauce over the nuts and seeds and toss well to coat.

NUT & SEED BUTTER

Read the labels of many commercial peanut butters and you will find sugar, palm oil, salt and preservatives, often in significant amounts. Home-made alternatives are quick and simple to make – and you choose the ingredients. This version uses a cold-pressed omega-blend oil that incorporates brain-boosting omega-3, -6 and -9. Find it in health-food shops and some supermarkets in the special diet section.

About 10 servings
30g/scant ⅓ cup unsalted cashews
30g/scant ⅓ cup blanched almonds
30g/scant ⅓ cup unsalted peanuts
1 tbsp pumpkin seeds
1 tbsp sunflower seeds
3 tbsp omega-blend or sunflower oil
1–2 tbsp olive oil
½ tsp salt

1 Lightly toast the nuts and seeds in a dry frying pan over medium-high heat for 3 minutes, stirring frequently, until golden. Leave to cool and remove the brown papery covering from any peanuts, if necessary.
2 Place the toasted nuts and seeds, the oils and salt in a food processor and blend until fairly smooth and creamy. Transfer to a jar and store in the refrigerator.

COOL DOGS

A nifty alternative to the high-fat, often poor quality sausage roll, the cool dog is made using high-meat, good quality sausages and a warm soft tortilla – simple and quick! This is a good example of a meal that is as good as its ingredients. Use the best sausages that you can find and you won't be filling your children with unwanted additives. And if you're using shop-bought bottled sauces to serve, look out for the 'no added sugar and salt' varieties.

RED PEPPER HUMOUS

Humous is far more versatile than its usual use as a dip. It also makes a nutritious addition to soups, stews and pasta sauces. The roasted red pepper in this recipe adds a delicious smoky sweetness as well as the beneficial antioxidants vitamin C and beta-carotene.

About 10 servings
1 small red pepper, seeded and cut
  into thick strips
3 tbsp extra-virgin olive oil
230g/8oz can 'no added salt and
  sugar' chickpeas, drained and rinsed
2 garlic cloves, crushed
1 tbsp light tahini
1 tbsp warm water
juice of ½ lemon
salt and pepper, to taste

1 Preheat the oven to 200°C/400°F. Place the pepper in a roasting pan with 1 tbsp oil and mix well to ensure the pepper is completely coated. Roast for 35–40 minutes until tender and the skin begins to blister. Transfer the pepper to a plastic bag or wrap in foil, and leave to cool. When the pepper is cool enough to handle, remove from the bag or foil and rub off the skin.
2 Place the pepper strips, chickpeas, garlic, tahini, water, lemon juice and remaining oil in a food processor or blender and purée until smooth. Season to taste.

Serves 2
4 good quality pork sausages or
  vegetarian alternative
1 small soft flour tortilla, cut into
  4 strips
Mayonnaise, ketchup, guacamole or
  humous, to serve

1 Preheat the grill to medium-high. Line a grill pan with foil and arrange the sausages on top. Grill the sausages until cooked through and golden.
2 Place the tortilla strips in a dry frying pan and heat until warmed through. When the sausages are cooked, lay them on the tortilla strips, add some mayonnaise, ketchup, guacamole or humous and serve.

BRAIN BOX

Chickpeas provide a good mix of brain-enhancing minerals, including magnesium, iron, phosphorus, zinc and manganese, necessary for constructing the brain's messengers.

TUNA TORTILLA MELT

Soft, floury tortillas are perfect for filling with all manner of healthy goodies. If you can find wholewheat versions, all the better. You could also use wholewheat pitta bread for this.

Serves 1–2
100g/½ cup canned tuna in spring
   water or olive oil, drained
1 large soft tortilla
30g/¼ cup grated mature Cheddar
1 small tomato, sliced

BRAIN BOX

Tuna is one of the oily fish family providing omega-3 fats, essential for brain development and function. Although the canned variety is lower in these beneficial oils than fresh tuna, it still makes a convenient protein food.

1 Mash the drained tuna with a fork and arrange it in the centre of the tortilla. Top with the grated Cheddar and sliced tomato.

2 Fold in the edges of the tortilla to encase the filling. Heat a dry, non-stick frying pan over medium heat. Place the tortilla, seam-side down, in the pan and cook for 3 minutes until warmed through and golden. Cut in half diagonally and serve.

GET-SMART TOASTIES

Fresh sardines are incredibly bony so tend not to be popular with children. However, the tinned variety is a useful alternative. Furthermore, the sardines are mixed with fresh tomato and pesto to dilute the fishy flavour.

Serves 2
2 slices wholemeal bread
1 can boned sardines in tomato sauce
3 heaped tsp fresh red pesto
1 tomato, seeded and chopped

1 Preheat the grill to medium-high. Line a grill pan with foil. Cut one slice of bread into a fish shape either freehand or using a cutter, incorporating as much of the bread as possible to reduce wastage. Repeat with the other slice of bread.

2 Mash the sardines and mix with the pesto and tomato.

3 Toast one side of each fish-shaped piece of bread, then turn over and lightly toast the other side. Spoon the sardine mixture on top and grill for 3 minutes until heated through.

BRAIN BOX

Oily fish, such as **canned sardines**, provide beneficial brain oils, which have been found to increase brain capacity, improving memory and concentration.

FRUITY EGGY BUN

French toast (also known as 'eggy bread'), works just as well when made with fruit bread, brioche or fruit buns and makes a quick comforting snack.

Serves 2
2 small wholemeal fruit buns, split in
   half
1 egg, beaten, mixed with 2 tbsp milk
25g/¼ stick unsalted butter

Dip each bun half into the egg-and-milk mixture until evenly covered. Melt the butter in a heavy-based frying pan and add the egg-soaked buns. Cook for 1–2 minutes on each side until the egg has set and is golden.

PIZZA POWER

All kids love pizza and home-made versions offer a good range of nutrients. This speedy version is perfect for hungry tummies that require filling in next to no time.

Serves 2

2 wholemeal muffins, split in half

4 tsp red pesto

1 tomato, seeded and chopped

4 slices mozzarella

1 Preheat the grill to medium-high. Line a grill pan with foil. Lightly toast the uncut side of each muffin half.

2 Mix together the pesto and tomato and spoon on top of the untoasted side of each muffin half. Top with the mozzarella and return to the grill for 3–5 minutes until melted and bubbling. Leave to cool slightly before serving.

BRAIN BOX

Mozzarella is a valuable low-fat protein food which, when combined with the muffins (a source of complex carbohydrate), will provide plenty of long-term energy.

MAIN MEALS

The recipes found in this section are perfect for weekday meals when your time in the kitchen may be limited. Full of goodness and very tasty, they will appeal to children and adults alike.

MIGHTY MINESTRONE

This adaptation of the popular Italian soup contains a plethora of beneficial brain foods from vegetables and beans to pasta and cheese. It tastes even better when made in advance. Serve with slices of garlic bread to boost carbohydrate intake.

Serves 4
2 tbsp olive oil
1 leek, sliced
1 carrot, finely chopped
1 stick celery, finely chopped
3 string beans, finely sliced
900ml/3¾ cups vegetable stock
300ml/1¼ cups passata
2 bay leaves
100g/scant 1 cup conchigliette (small
    shells) pasta
100g/⅔ cup canned cannellini beans,
    drained and rinsed
sprig of fresh rosemary
salt and pepper, to taste
freshly grated Parmesan, to serve

1 Heat the oil in a large heavy-based saucepan over medium heat and add the leek. Cook for 5 minutes, stirring occasionally, until tender. Add the carrot, celery and string beans and cook for a further 5 minutes.
2 Pour in the stock and passata and add the bay leaves, stir well. Bring to the boil, then reduce the heat and simmer, half-covered, for 15 minutes. Remove the bay leaves and, using a

BRAIN BOX

Beans contain B-group vitamins, iron, zinc and magnesium, all of which are vital for brain function, memory and a healthy nervous system.

hand-blender (or food processor), purée the vegetables slightly, so that there are still some bits of vegetable in the soup.
3 Return the bay leaves to the soup, add the pasta, beans and rosemary and bring to the boil. Reduce the heat slightly and cook for 10 minutes or until the pasta is tender. Remove the bay leaves and rosemary and season to taste. You may need to add extra stock or water if the soup seems too thick.
4 Divide between four bowls and serve with a sprinkling of Parmesan.

TOMATO & LENTIL SOUP

Tomato soup is a perennial favourite but shop-bought versions contain a surprising amount of fat, sugar and salt, and the canning process depletes vital nutrients. This nutritious home-made version features the added health benefit of lentils and doesn't take an age to make. Serve with hunks of crusty bread.

BRAIN BOX

Recent research shows that lycopene, the pigment that turns tomatoes red, is a powerful antioxidant, protecting the brain and nervous system from destructive free radicals. Luckily, **cooked tomatoes** are just as nutritious as fresh ones.

Lentils contain the important brain combo of iron, B-group vitamins and zinc.

Serves 4
50g/¼ cup dried split red lentils, rinsed
1 tbsp olive oil
1 onion, chopped
1 carrot, finely chopped
1 stick celery, finely chopped
500ml/2 cups passata
500ml/2 cups vegetable stock
1 bay leaf
salt and pepper, to taste
3 tbsp milk

1 Place the lentils in a saucepan, cover with water and bring to the boil. Reduce the heat and simmer, half-covered, for 15 minutes or until just tender. Using a slotted spoon, remove any scum that rises to the surface using a spoon. Drain the lentils well and set aside.
2 Meanwhile, heat the oil in a large heavy-based saucepan over medium heat. Add the onion, cover the pan and sweat for 8 minutes until softened and transparent. Add the carrot and celery, cover, and cook for a further 3 minutes, stirring occasionally to prevent the vegetables sticking to the bottom of the pan.
3 Add the passata, stock, lentils and bay leaf. Bring to the boil. Reduce the heat and simmer, half-covered, for 25 minutes until the lentils and vegetables are tender and the soup has thickened.

4 Carefully pour the soup into a blender or use a hand blender to purée the soup until smooth. Return to the pan, season to taste and stir in the milk. Reheat, if necessary, and serve.

CHICKEN NOODLE SOUP

If time is short, this nutritious miso soup is just the thing. It's simple to make and contains calm-inducing carbohydrates in the form of noodles and protein-rich mini chicken dumplings. You can find sachets of miso soup in health-food shops and some supermarkets.

Serves 2
100g/scant 1 cup medium egg noodles
1 pak choi, halved
2 sachets instant miso soup
2 tsp soy sauce
1 small carrot, cut into fine sticks
1 spring onion, cut into fine slivers
sesame seeds, for sprinkling

for the chicken dumplings:
150g/⅔ cup minced chicken
1 small egg
½ tsp cornflour
½ tsp paprika
1 tsp ground coriander
1 spring onion, finely chopped
salt and pepper, to taste

BRAIN BOX

Miso soup is made from a mixture of soy beans and rice, wheat or barley. It has a cleansing, rejuvenating effect on the body, helping it to get rid of toxins which can cloud the brain.

Chicken is a high-protein food that helps to focus the mind.

1 To make the chicken dumplings, combine the ingredients in a bowl until well mixed. Bring a pan of water to the boil. Using two teaspoons, form the chicken mixture into small balls, then drop them into the boiling water. Cook the balls, a few at a time, for 5 minutes until cooked through. Keep the cooked dumplings warm.

2 Meanwhile, cook the noodles in boiling water for about 5 minutes or until tender, adding the pak choi 2 minutes before the end of the cooking time. Drain well and slice the pak choi.

3 Dilute the miso soup according to packet instructions. Add the soy sauce and stir well.

4 To serve, divide the noodles between two bowls, pour over the miso soup. Stir in the pak choi, carrot and spring onion. Sprinkle with the sesame seeds and arrange the chicken dumplings on top.

RÖSTI NESTS

The carbohydrates provided by the potatoes help to boost serotonin levels, the brain calming chemical – making this a perfect meal for the end of the day. An egg nestles in the centre of each rösti for extra goodness. Serve with a green vegetable of your choice.

Serves 2
275g/9½oz potatoes, halved
1 large carrot, cut into three pieces
salt and pepper, to taste
sunflower oil, for frying
2 eggs

1 Steam the potatoes and carrot for 10 minutes until just tender but not completely cooked. Leave to cool, then peel the potatoes and coarsely grate them and the carrot into a bowl.

2 Season the potato mixture and divide into two. Shape each half into a ring with a hole in the centre – they are quite fragile but will firm up when cooked.

3 Pre-heat the grill to medium. Pour enough oil to just cover the bottom into a heavy-based frying pan and warm over medium-high heat. Carefully place the rösti in the pan and cook for 7 minutes on one side until golden, then turn it over and cook for a further 5 minutes. Break an egg into the hole in the centre of each rösti and cook for a further 2 minutes.

4 Place the frying pan under the preheated grill and cook the rösti for another 2 minutes or until the egg is just set, and serve.

EGGS FLORENTINE

It can be a challenge to encourage children to eat green vegetables but here the creamy sauce helps to make the spinach more palatable. Serve this dish with pasta, rice or bread.

Serves 2
225g/4¼ cups young leaf spinach, washed and rinsed well
3 tbsp double cream or crème fraîche
a little grated nutmeg
2 eggs
40g/⅓ cup grated mature Cheddar cheese

1 Steam the spinach for a few minutes until tender. Leave to drain, then squeeze out any further water using your hands. Finely chop the spinach, then mix with the cream and a little grated nutmeg in a small pan and cook until heated through. Then spoon the spinach into a small ovenproof dish.
2 Make two holes in the spinach mixture, large enough to accommodate the eggs. Break the eggs into the holes, top the eggs with the grated cheese and grill for 2–3 minutes until the eggs have set.

BRAIN BOX

B-group vitamins found in **eggs** are essential for optimum brain functioning, particularly clarity of thought.

The vitamin C in the **spinach** helps the absorption of the iron also found in this green vegetable. Iron helps boost energy levels.

HIGH-ENERGY BEAN BURGERS

Cheap meat-based burgers offer little in the way of nourishment and are high in fat and additives. These veggie-versions take a little more effort but provide numerous health benefits.

Makes 4 burgers
120g/scant ⅔ cup canned kidney beans, drained and rinsed
½ onion, grated
1 small carrot, grated
40g/⅔ cup fresh wholemeal breadcrumbs
1 tbsp smooth peanut butter
1 egg, beaten
salt and pepper, to taste
flour, for coating
sunflower oil, for frying
4 wholemeal burger buns or seedy bagels, to serve
shredded lettuce, tomato and cucumber slices, to serve

1 Put the kidney beans in a food processor or blender with the onion, carrot, breadcrumbs, peanut butter and egg. Blend until the mixture forms a coarse purée. Season, then chill for 1 hour to allow the mixture to firm up.
2 Form the mixture into four burgers using floured hands, then dip each burger into flour to coat.
3 Heat enough oil to just cover the bottom of a large, heavy-based frying pan. Cook the burgers, two at a time, for about 3 minutes each side or until golden and crisp. Drain on paper towels. (To grill the burgers, brush with oil and grill for about 4 minutes on each side.) Repeat with the remaining burgers.
4 To serve, split each burger bun or bagel in half. Add the burgers and lettuce, tomato and cucumber, as liked. Serve with a spoonful of humous, guacamole or tomato ketchup.

DREAMY CHINESE RICE

Parents will welcome this lightly spiced rice dish. Brown rice is a complex carbohydrate and as such will instill feelings of sleepiness and calmness – well that's the theory! The rice is topped with strips of omelette.

Serves 2
2 tsp sunflower oil
splash of toasted sesame oil
1 garlic clove, chopped
½ tsp Chinese five spice
¼ red pepper, seeded and diced
4 baby corn, cut into rounds
4 small broccoli florets
1 spring onion, sliced diagonally
small knob of fresh root ginger, peeled
    and grated (optional)
60ml/¼ cup fresh apple juice (not
    concentrate)
2 tbsp stock or water
300g/scant 2 cups cold, cooked brown
    rice
2 tsp soy sauce
1 tsp sesame seeds

WARNING

It is important to make sure that the **cooked rice** has been heated through thoroughly before serving. Cooked rice that has been reheated inadequately is a surprisingly common source of food poisoning.

for the omelette:
small knob of butter
1 egg, beaten

1 Heat the sunflower and sesame oils in a wok or heavy-based frying pan. Add the garlic, Chinese five spice, red pepper, baby corn, broccoli, spring onion and ginger (if liked) and stir-fry for 4 minutes.
2 Add the apple juice and water and stir-fry for another 3 minutes or until the vegetables are tender.
3 Add the rice and soy sauce to the wok and stir until thoroughly warmed through. Mix in the sesame seeds.

4 To make the omelette, melt the butter in a small frying pan and add the egg. Swirl the egg until it covers the base of the pan. Cook until the egg has set, then turn out onto a plate. Cut into strips.
5 To serve, divide the rice between two bowls and arrange the omelette strips on top.

NICE-RICE & VEG FRITTERS

These are easy to prepare and make use of leftover brown rice. Serve them with low-sugar and low-salt baked beans or steamed green vegetables.

BRAIN BOX

Complex carbohydrates (here, in **brown rice**) have a soothing effect on the mind since they stimulate the release of the calming chemical serotonin in the brain. They also provide plenty of long-term energy, keeping blood-sugar levels steady, which is important for a good night's sleep. Brown rice also contains B-group vitamins, essential for healthy brain function.

Makes 8 fritters

100g/heaping ⅔ cup cold cooked brown rice
1 small leek, finely chopped
½ yellow pepper, seeded and finely diced
1 garlic clove, crushed
2 tbsp freshly grated Parmesan
1 small egg, beaten
2 tbsp double cream
2 tbsp flour
salt and pepper, to taste
sunflower oil, for frying

1 Mix together the rice, leek, yellow pepper, garlic, Parmesan, egg, cream and flour in a bowl to make a sloppy batter. Season to taste.

2 Heat enough oil to lightly coat the bottom of a heavy-based frying pan. Place two heaped dessertspoons of the rice mixture per fritter into the hot oil and flatten slightly with a spatula. Cook in batches for 3 minutes on each side until golden. Drain on kitchen towels before serving.

VEGETABLE & TOFU KEBABS
WITH A SATAY DIP

A powerhouse of brain nutrients are provided by these colourful vegetable kebabs which are served with a peanut dipping sauce. These kebabs also make a good vegetarian addition – for children or adults – to a barbecue. Serve with a warm tortilla or naan bread. The satay dip will keep for up to a week if stored in the refrigerator.

Makes 4 kebabs
130g/4¾oz tofu, cut into 8 cubes
2 courgette, cut into 8 chunks
4 cherry tomatoes
¼ yellow pepper, cut into 4 chunks

for the marinade:
1 tbsp runny honey
1 tsp soy sauce
1 tbsp toasted sesame oil
1 tsp olive oil
1 garlic clove, sliced

for the satay dip:
2 tbsp smooth peanut butter
1 tsp olive oil
1 tsp hot water
1 tsp soy sauce
½ tsp light muscovado sugar
2 tbsp mayonnaise

1 To make the marinade, mix together the ingredients in a shallow non-metallic dish. Put the tofu, courgette, cherry tomatoes and pepper in the marinade. Cover with clingfilm and leave to marinate for at least 1 hour or preferably overnight, turning the vegetables and tofu occasionally.
2 Place four wooden skewers in a bowl of water and leave to soak for 30 minutes – this helps to prevent the skewers burning. Meanwhile, to make the satay dip, combine the ingredients in a small bowl and mix together well.
3 Preheat the grill to medium-high. Line the grill pan with foil. Arrange the tofu and vegetables on the soaked skewers, reserving the marinade: place a piece of courgette, then a tofu cube,

Vitamin C found in **sweet peppers, tomatoes and courgettes** aids the absorption of minerals such as iron.

Tofu is a low-fat protein, rich in minerals, particularly iron, magnesium and calcium, important nutrients for a healthy nervous system and brain.

a cherry tomato, chunk of pepper, another tofu cube and finally another piece of courgette on each skewer. Repeat to make three more kebabs.
4 Arrange the kebabs on the grill pan. Brush with the reserved marinade. Grill for 8–10 minutes, turning occasionally and brushing with the marinade, until golden. Serve with the satay dip.

QUICK TOMATO PASTA

Encouraging children to eat vegetables is an on-going challenge and while it's important to promote a love of vegetables, attempts don't always work. This pasta sauce – with its sneaky hidden vegetables – is very popular with my kids.

Serves 2
115g/4oz wholewheat spaghetti
freshly grated Parmesan, to serve

for the sauce:
1 tbsp olive oil
1 small onion, finely chopped
½ red pepper, seeded and diced
1 large garlic clove, crushed
1 tsp dried oregano
1 carrot, finely chopped
300ml/1¼ cups passata
1 tsp tomato purée
¼ tsp caster sugar (optional)
salt and pepper, to taste

1 Heat the oil in a medium-sized heavy-based saucepan over medium heat and cook the onion for 7 minutes, half-covered, until softened. Add the red pepper and cook for a further 3 minutes, half-covered, stirring frequently. Add the garlic and oregano and cook for 1 minute. Meanwhile, steam the carrot for 5 minutes until just tender.

2 Pour in the passata, then stir in the tomato purée, sugar (if using) and carrot, season and cook for 8 minutes over a low heat until reduced and thickened. Purée the sauce in a food processor until smooth and creamy.
3 Meanwhile, cook the pasta following the packet instructions. Drain, reserving 2 tablespoons of the cooking water. Combine the pasta, cooking liquid and sauce. Serve sprinkled with Parmesan.

BACON & PEA PENNE

Try to buy good quality bacon for the best flavour and health benefits. For extra goodness serve this dish with steamed broccoli.

Serves 2
2 rashers of back bacon
115g/1 cup penne pasta
1 tbsp olive oil
1 large garlic clove, chopped
125ml/½ cup vegetable stock
75g/¾ cup frozen peas
3 tbsp crème fraîche
salt and pepper, to taste
freshly grated Parmesan, to serve

1 Remove the rind from the bacon and grill until crisp. Cook the pasta in boiling water following the packet instructions. Drain, reserving about 1 tablespoon of the cooking water.
2 Meanwhile, heat the olive oil in a heavy-based frying pan over medium-high heat and fry the garlic for 1 minute until softened. Add the stock and the peas and cook for 2 minutes until the peas are cooked and the liquid has reduced.
3 Cut the bacon into small pieces and add to the pan with the crème fraîche. Cook over a low heat, stirring frequently, until warmed through. Stir the pasta and reserved water into the sauce and mix gently until combined. Season to taste and serve sprinkled with Parmesan.

BRAIN BOX

Peas are little nuggets of goodness, providing plenty of vitamin C and B-group vitamins as well as zinc, a nutrient that aids concentration. This even applies to frozen peas, which can be more nutritious than fresh, if the latter have been stored for some time.

Bacon also provides B vitamins, essential for the health of the nervous system.

SALMON STICKS

The marinade gives these salmon kebabs a wonderful sweet, glossy glaze. A certain amount of forward planning is required as they need to marinate for at least an hour to absorb the flavours of the marinade. While kebabs are fun, do take care with the skewers when giving them to children. They are served with a fruity couscous, and you can add a green vegetable for extra health benefits.

Serves 2
150g/5oz salmon fillet, skinned and
   cut into 16 cubes

for the marinade:
1 tbsp runny honey
2 tsp soy sauce
1 tsp omega-blend oil or olive oil
1 tsp toasted sesame oil
1 garlic clove, sliced

for the fruity couscous:
55g/¼ cup couscous
vegetable stock, for soaking
small knob of butter
½ nectarine or peach, diced
1 tbsp toasted sesame seeds
1 tbsp toasted flaked almonds

1 Mix together the ingredients for the marinade in a shallow, non-metallic dish. Add the cubes of salmon and turn until the fish is coated in the marinade. Cover with clingfilm and leave to marinate in the refrigerator for at least 1 hour, preferably overnight, turning the fish occasionally.
2 To make the couscous, pour the couscous grains into a heatproof bowl. Bring the vegetable stock to a boil and pour enough into the bowl to just

cover the couscous – there should be about 5mm (¼in) of stock above the couscous. Leave until the grains have absorbed all of the liquid. Add a small knob of butter and fluff up with a fork. Stir in the diced nectarine, seeds and nuts and set aside.

3 Meanwhile, soak four wooden skewers in a bowl of water for 30 minutes to prevent them burning. Preheat the grill to high and line the grill pan with foil. Thread the cubes of salmon on to the skewers and brush with the marinade. Grill the kebabs for 3–5 minutes, turning halfway through and brushing with more marinade, until cooked through. Serve with the fruity couscous.

FANTASTIC FAJITAS

Add a taste of Mexico to tea-time with these healthy prawn-filled tortillas. Serve with a green salad or chunks of pepper, carrot and cucumber to dip into creamy avocado dip (see page 57) or red pepper humous (see page 59).

Serves 2
1 tbsp olive oil
1 garlic clove, chopped
½ red pepper, seeded and
   cut into strips
150ml/⅔ cup passata
½ tsp ground cumin
1 tbsp tomato purée
juice of ½ lime
115g/4oz cooked prawns, defrosted
   if frozen

2 small soft tortillas
½ small avocado, stoned, peeled and
   diced, to serve
spoonfuls of crème fraîche, fromage
   frais or natural yogurt, to serve

1 Heat the olive oil in a heavy-based frying pan over a medium-low heat and fry the garlic and red pepper for 3 minutes until softened. Add the passata, cumin and tomato purée and cook for 8 minutes over a medium heat until reduced and thickened. Add the lime juice and stir in the prawns, heat well.

2 Warm the tortillas, then spoon the prawn mixture on one side of each one. Top the filling with the diced avocado and spoon the crème fraîche or other topping on top. Fold the tortillas over to encase the filling and serve.

BRAIN BOX

Prawns contain an amino acid, called tyrosine, which helps to increase alertness, as well as zinc, a crucial brain mineral that helps to control mood swings and irritability.

SALMON FINGERS WITH SWEET POTATO CHIPS

This healthy version of the children's classic fish fingers and chips offers plenty of mind-stimulating nutrients. If making your own sounds a bit of a faff, be reassured that these salmon fingers are quick and easy to make. Peas are a must as an accompaniment.

Serves 2–3
200g/7oz salmon fillet, skinned
75g/¾ cup fine cornmeal or polenta
2 tbsp freshly grated Parmesan
1 egg, beaten
sunflower oil, for frying
salt and pepper, to taste

for the sweet potato chips:
1 small sweet potato, scrubbed and cut into wedges
2 tsp olive oil

1 Preheat the oven to 200°C/400°F. To make the chips, dry the sweet potatoes on a clean tea towel. Spoon the oil into a roasting tin and heat briefly. Toss the sweet potatoes in the warm oil until covered and roast for 30 minutes, turning them halfway through, until tender and golden.
2 Meanwhile, cut the salmon into six thick finger shapes. Mix together the cornmeal or polenta with the Parmesan on a plate. Dip each salmon finger into the beaten egg then roll them in the cornmeal and Parmesan mixture until evenly coated.
3 Pour enough oil into a large heavy-based frying pan to cover the base and warm over medium high heat. Carefully arrange the salmon fingers in the pan and cook them for 6 minutes, turning halfway through, until golden. Drain on kitchen paper, season, then serve with the sweet potato chips.

 BRAIN BOX

Sweet potatoes, particularly the orange-fleshed variety, provide the antioxidants vitamin C and beta-carotene, which help to enhance memory.

SUPER-FISH!

This simple fish supper couldn't be easier to make but looks great – and for those kids who are not big fans of fish, the mozzarella, pesto and tomato topping add plenty of colour and flavour. Serve with new potatoes and corn on the cob.

Serves 2
2 x 150g/5oz cod fillets, skinned
olive oil, for brushing
2 heaped tsp red or green pesto
1 tomato, sliced and seeded
2 slices mozzarella
salt and pepper, to taste

1 Preheat the grill to high and line a grill pan with foil. Check the cod for any bones that remain and remove. Brush both sides of each fillet with the oil. Place the fish in the grill pan and grill for 3 minutes, turn and cook for a further 2–3 minutes until opaque and just cooked through.
2 Remove the pan from the grill and arrange a heaped spoonful of pesto on top of each fillet. Arrange the tomato slices then the mozzarella on top of the pesto. Grill for 3–4 minutes until the mozzarella has melted and is turning slightly golden. Season and serve.

EASY-PEASY FISH PIE

This fish pie packs a powerful punch when it comes to brain-nurturing nutrients. It cuts a few corners when it comes to preparation in that it gets its creaminess from crème fraîche rather than a white sauce. Steamed broccoli or string beans go particularly well with this dish.

Serves 2
225g/8oz cod fillet, skinned
85g/3oz undyed smoked haddock
   fillet, skinned
milk, for poaching
2 tsp olive oil
1 garlic clove, chopped
1 small leek, sliced
75g/¾ cup frozen peas
100ml/scant ½ cup half-fat crème
   fraîche
1 tsp Dijon mustard
1 tbsp snipped fresh chives
1 egg, hard-boiled and quartered

BRAIN BOX

Cod is a good source of low-fat protein as well as some B-group vitamins, selenium and vitamin E, all nutrients necessary for healthy brain function.

for the mash:
500g/1lb 2oz potatoes, peeled and
   cut into chunks
1 tbsp olive oil
2 tbsp butter
60ml/¼ cup warm milk or the milk
   used to poach the fish
salt and pepper, to taste

1 To make the mash, cook the potatoes in boiling water for 15–20 minutes until tender. Drain well.
2 Meanwhile, place the fish in a frying pan and just cover with milk. Poach the fish for 8 minutes or until just cooked. Remove the fish from the poaching liquid and flake into large chunks, removing any stray bones.

3 Heat the oil in a large heavy-based frying pan and fry the garlic and leek for 5 minutes. Add the peas and cook briefly, stirring constantly. Stir in the crème fraîche and mustard. Cook until heated through and carefully stir in the chives, hard-boiled egg and cooked fish. Spoon the mixture into a heatproof dish.
4 Preheat the grill to medium. Drain the potatoes well and add the olive oil, butter and warm milk (or fish-poaching milk). Mash until smooth and creamy and spoon over the fish. Smooth the mashed potato slightly and place the dish under the grill for 3–5 minutes until the top becomes golden.

CHICKEN & COCONUT NOODLES

Strips of chicken top the Malaysian-inspired coconut noodles in this dish. Prawns or lean pork make tasty, nutritious alternatives to the chicken and the selection of vegetables can be adapted to suit personal tastes.

Serves 2

175g/6oz skinless boneless chicken breast, cut into thin strips
115g/1 cup medium egg noodles
1 tbsp sunflower oil
1 small leek, sliced
1 garlic clove, chopped
¼ red pepper, seeded and diced
1 small courgette, diced
4 baby corn, sliced lengthways
6 mangetout
1 tsp mild curry powder
150ml/⅔ cup coconut milk
100ml/scant ½ cup vegetable stock
sesame seeds and sliced spring onion, to serve (optional)

1 Preheat the grill to high and line the grill pan with foil. Brush the chicken with a little of the oil and grill for 8 minutes or until golden and cooked through; keep warm.

2 While the chicken is being grilled, cook the noodles according to the packet instructions. Drain well and rinse under cold running water to prevent them cooking further. Leave to drain thoroughly.

3 Heat the remaining oil in a wok and stir-fry the leek, garlic, red pepper, courgette, baby corn and mangetout for 5 minutes, tossing the vegetables frequently. Add the curry powder and cook for another minute.

BRAIN BOX

Chicken is high in good quality protein as well as selenium, zinc and B-group vitamins. The skin is full of saturated fat so it is important to remove it. Buy organic poultry if you can to avoid unwanted chemicals that may affect brain efficiency.

4 Add the coconut milk and stock and cook for 5 minutes until the liquid has reduced and thickened. Add the noodles to heat though.

5 To serve, spoon the noodles, veg and sauce into bowls, top with the chicken strips and sprinkle with sesame seeds and spring onion, if liked.

GREAT BALLS OF ... CHICKEN!

A great Italian-inspired dish that's popular with kids. Serve it with pasta or rice and a green vegetable or salad.

Serves 2

250g/heaping 1 cup minced chicken
2 tbsp freshly grated Parmesan
25g/½ cup fresh breadcrumbs
1 small egg, beaten
salt and pepper, to taste
sunflower oil, for frying

for the tomato sauce:
1 garlic clove, crushed
½ tsp dried oregano
300ml/1¼ cups passata
pinch of sugar

1 To make the meatballs, mix together the chicken, Parmesan, breadcrumbs and egg. Season lightly and form into 10 small balls using two dessertspoons – they don't have to be perfectly round since the mixture is quite moist.

2 Heat enough oil to just cover the bottom of a heavy-based frying pan and cook the balls for 6–8 minutes, turning occasionally, until golden and cooked though. Remove from the pan and keep warm.

3 To make the sauce, put the garlic and oregano in the pan, adding a little more oil if necessary. Fry for 1 minute then add the passata and a pinch of sugar. Cook for 4 minutes over a medium-low heat, stirring occasionally.

4 Return the chicken balls to the pan and cook for a further 4 minutes until heated through and the sauce has reduced and thickened.

MAGIC MINCE WITH APRICOTS

This mildly spiced mince dish is magic in that it provides a potent range of essential brain nutrients from iron and betacarotene to B-group vitamins. Serve the mince with a jacket potato and green vegetables.

Serves 2

1 tbsp olive oil
1 small onion, finely chopped
1 garlic clove, chopped
1 small carrot, grated
½ small red pepper, seeded and diced
140g/scant ⅔ cup lean minced beef or
    vegetarian alternative
¼ tsp ground cumin
½ tsp ground cinnamon
¼ tsp ground coriander
250ml/1 cup passata
125ml/½ cup chicken or vegetable
    stock
1 tbsp tomato purée
6 ready-to-eat unsulphured dried
    apricots
salt and pepper, to taste

1 Heat the oil in a large heavy-based saucepan over medium heat, add the onion and cook, covered, stirring occasionally, for 7 minutes until softened and tender. Add the garlic, carrot and pepper and cook, covered, for a further 3 minutes.

2 Push the contents of the pan to one side and add the mince. Cook, uncovered, stirring frequently until browned. Stir in the spices and cook for another minute.

3 Pour in the passata and stock and add the tomato purée and apricots. Stir well and cook, half-covered, for 30 minutes until reduced and thickened. If the sauce appears too liquid remove the lid, or if is it too dry add a little more stock. Season to taste and serve.

BRAIN BOX

Many shy away from **red meat** for various reasons but it does have a role to play in the brain-food diet, providing all eight essential amino acids necessary to make neurotransmitters. It is also a good source of iron, which plays a role in aiding memory and learning. Make sure you buy lean organic meat.

WEEKEND MEALS

The following recipes might take a little longer to prepare – but they are worth it! Don't be afraid to be adventurous, the wide range of ingredients used will give the whole family the opportunity to appreciate all sorts of different flavours.

SLEEPYTIME CHEESY PASTA

A cheese sauce can be invaluable for making vegetables more acceptable to children. Additionally, if your children are like coiled springs at the end of the day, a helping of pasta enveloped in a creamy cheese sauce may help to calm them down.

Serves 4
175g/1½ cups penne pasta, preferably
　　wholemeal
175g/6oz broccoli, cut into small
　　florets
85g/3oz cauliflower, cut into small
　　florets
1 large leek, sliced
25g/¼ stick butter
3 tbsp plain flour
750ml/3 cups milk, warmed
1 tsp dried oregano (optional)
1 tbsp Dijon mustard
120g/1 cup grated mature Cheddar
　　cheese, plus extra for sprinkling
2 tbsp fresh wholemeal breadcrumbs

1 Cook the pasta in plenty of boiling salted water following the packet instructions. Meanwhile, steam the broccoli, cauliflower and leek for 5–7 minutes until tender. Drain the pasta and transfer to an ovenproof dish with the vegetables.
2 To make the cheese sauce, melt the butter in a heavy-based saucepan. Reduce the heat and stir in the flour and cook for about 2 minutes, stirring

BRAIN BOX

Both **broccoli and cauliflower** belong to the cruciferous family of vegetables and provide potent antioxidants, helping to protect the brain from harmful free radicals.

continuously with a wooden spoon until the mixture forms a thick light brown paste. Gradually add the warm milk, whisking well with a balloon whisk. Continue to add the milk and cook until the mixture has thickened and formed a silky, creamy sauce.
3 Add the oregano, if using, mustard and cheese and heat, stirring, until the cheese has melted. Pour the sauce over the pasta and vegetables and stir gently until combined.
4 Preheat the grill to medium-high. Sprinkle the pasta with extra grated cheese and breadcrumbs and grill until the cheese has melted and the breadcrumbs are golden.

BEANZ MEANZ BRAINS

Tofu is made from the highly nutritious soya bean, which is rich in high-quality, low-fat protein since it contains all eight essential amino acids. Tofu benefits from being combined with stronger flavours, as in these lightly spiced tofu cakes. They're excellent with a dollop of mango chutney, brown rice and a salad for a light lunch or with the noodle salad (see page 82).

Makes 10 cakes
240g/8½oz tofu, grated
1 small onion, grated
1 carrot, finely grated
½ tsp lemon juice
1 tsp ground cumin
2–3 tsp curry paste of your choice
75g/⅓ cup plain flour, plus extra for
　　dusting
sunflower oil, for brushing
salt and pepper, to taste

1 Place the tofu, onion, carrot, lemon juice, cumin and curry paste in a non-metallic bowl, combine well and marinate for at least an hour to allow the flavour of the spices to infuse the tofu.
2 Preheat the grill to medium and line the grill pan with foil. Stir in the flour until well mixed and season with salt and pepper. Shape the mixture into 10 cakes. Brush the cakes with oil and grill for 3 minutes. Turn them over, brush with more oil and cook for a further 3 minutes until golden. Serve.

CHICKPEA & AUBERGINE TAGINE

The sweetness of the dried apricots add to the popularity of this tasty vegetable and bean stew. Grilling the aubergine first helps to keep fat levels down, since aubergines are prone to absorbing a lot of oil when fried. Serve the tagine with plain couscous. Adults may like to add some chilli!

Serves 4

1 tbsp olive oil, plus extra for brushing
1 large onion, chopped
1 carrot, diced
1 large aubergine, cut into bite-sized
  pieces
1 red pepper, sliced
2 garlic cloves, chopped
1 tsp ground coriander
2 tsp ground cumin
1 tsp ground turmeric
600ml/2½ cups passata
100g/scant ½ cup vegetable stock
2 tsp tomato purée
10 ready-to-eat unsulphured apricots,
  chopped
200g/¾ cup canned chickpeas, drained
  and rinsed
handful of pitted black olives (optional)
salt and pepper, to taste
1 tbsp chopped fresh coriander, to
garnish (optional)

1 Heat the olive oil in a large heavy-based saucepan over medium heat, add the onion and cook, covered, for 7 minutes until softened. Steam the carrot for 3 minutes until just tender.
2 Meanwhile, preheat the grill to medium and line the grill pan with foil. Arrange the aubergine pieces on the foil and brush with the extra oil. Grill for 6 minutes, turning the aubergine occasionally, until browned and tender.

3 Add the pepper and garlic to the onion and cook, covered and stirring occasionally, for 2 minutes. Stir in the spices and cook for a further 1 minute.
4 Pour in the passata, stock and stir in the tomato purée and cook for 5 minutes, then add the apricots, chickpeas and olives, if using. Cook for 10 minutes, half-covered and stirring occasionally, until reduced and thickened. Season to taste and serve with couscous. Sprinkle with fresh coriander, if liked, just before serving.

BRAIN BOX

Vegetables, beans and grains should play a major part in a healthy diet. For the brain, these slow-releasing carbohydrates provide sustained amounts of energy and aid concentration. Beans are also a good source of B-group vitamins, iron, magnesium and zinc.

REVITALISING RICE

The combination of brown rice, lentils, eggs and vegetables provides a powerful protein punch. This lightly spiced dish always goes down well with my family. It's good served in a chapati or soft tortilla.

Serves 4–6

100g/½ cup dried red split lentils
200g/1 cup brown rice
1 tbsp olive oil
1 large onion, finely chopped
2 garlic cloves, crushed
1 tsp finely grated fresh root ginger
½ tsp ground turmeric
2–3 tsp garam masala
600ml/2½ cups vegetable stock
1 carrot, diced
3 string beans, sliced on the diagonal
115g/1 cup frozen peas
4 hard-boiled eggs, quartered
chapati or small soft tortilla, to serve (optional)

1 Rinse the lentils and rice separately under cold running water. Put the lentils in a pan and cover with cold water. Bring to the boil, then reduce the heat, skim off any foam that rises to the surface and cook, half-covered, for 20 minutes or until tender. Drain well and set aside.

2 Meanwhile, heat the oil in a large heavy-based saucepan and cook the onion, covered, for 7 minutes until softened. Add the garlic and ginger and cook for a further 1 minute. Stir in the spices and rice and cook for another minute.

3 Add the vegetable stock to the rice and bring to the boil, then reduce the heat, cover, and simmer for 15 minutes. Add the carrot and string

beans, stir and return the lid. Cook for a further 20 minutes until the rice is tender and all the water has been absorbed, adding the peas 5 minutes before the end of the cooking time.

4 Gently stir the lentils into the spicy rice until combined. Spoon on to a chapati or tortilla, and top each serving with a hard-boiled egg. The chapati or tortilla can be rolled up, if preferred.

CLEVER CASHEW ROASTS

Cashews contain a whole range of brain-nourishing nutrients, so although nut roasts have become a bit of a vegetarian cliché, they offer significant health benefits. This version is very light and comes with a creamy onion sauce. Serve with roast potatoes and steamed broccoli and sprouts.

Serves 4
2 tbsp olive oil
2 onions, finely chopped
2 carrots, grated
1 parsnip, grated
2 tsp dried mixed herbs
1 tsp thyme
140g/scant 1 cup unsalted cashew
   nuts
2 slices wholemeal bread, crusts
   removed
2 tbsp sunflower seeds
1 tbsp Worcestershire sauce (or
   vegetarian alternative)
1 tsp stock or bouillon powder
2 eggs, beaten
salt and pepper, to taste

for the onion sauce:
large knob of butter
1 tsp olive oil
2 onions, finely chopped
1 tbsp plain flour
300ml/1¼ cups milk, warmed
1 tsp Dijon mustard
good pinch of nutmeg
salt and pepper, to taste

1 To make the nut roast: preheat the oven to 200°C/400°F. Heat the oil in a large heavy-based saucepan, add the onion and cook, covered, for 7 minutes until softened. Add the carrots, parsnip and herbs and cook for a further 2 minutes. Remove the pan from the heat.
2 Meanwhile, grind the cashews in a food processor until finely chopped then process the bread into crumbs. Stir into the pan with the seeds, Worcestershire sauce and bouillon powder. Add the beaten eggs, season, and stir until combined.
3 Spoon the mixture into 4 individual greased dariole moulds or 10 cm (4 in) diameter ring moulds. Bake for 30 minutes until golden and crisp on top.
4 Meanwhile, make the onion sauce. Heat the butter and oil in a saucepan and cook the onions, covered, for 8 minutes until softened and beginning to brown. Add the flour, reduce the

heat, and stir continuously for 1 minute. Add half of the warm milk and cook over a medium-low heat, stirring, until it begins to thicken. Stir in the remaining milk and the mustard and cook for 6 minutes until it reaches a creamy consistency and there is no flouriness to the sauce. Season with the nutmeg and salt and pepper. Purée in a blender or food processor until smooth and creamy. Transfer to a pan and reheat if necessary.

TERIYAKI TUNA WITH NOODLES

Fresh tuna is part of the oily fish family and as such makes great brain food. It normally goes down well with children partly due to its firm, meaty texture and mild flavour. This dish comes with a light sesame noodle salad.

Serves 4
8 tbsp bottled teriyaki sauce
1 tsp honey
500g/1lb 2oz fresh tuna, cut into strips
salt and pepper, to taste
1 tsp sesame seeds, to serve (optional)

for the noodle salad:
200g/scant 2 cups medium egg
   noodles
3 tsp soy sauce
2 tsp sesame oil
1 tbsp olive oil
squeeze of lemon juice

> **BRAIN** BOX
>
> B-group vitamins, omega-6 essential fatty acids, calcium, iron, magnesium, potassium, selenium and zinc are among the plethora of brain-stimulating nutrients provided by **cashew nuts**. Cashews are, however, fairly high in fat and should be eaten in moderation.

½ tsp honey
4 tomatoes, seeded and chopped
5 cm/2 in length of cucumber, diced
½ red pepper, seeded and diced
1 tbsp chopped fresh coriander or basil
    (optional)
2 spring onions, sliced on the diagonal

1 Combine the teriyaki sauce and
honey and pour over the tuna. Turn
the tuna in the marinade to coat it.
Season with salt and pepper. Leave to
marinate for at least 1 hour, turning
the fish occasionally.
2 Meanwhile, to make the noodle
salad, cook the noodles according to
the packet instructions. Drain well and
rinse the noodles under cold running
water. Mix together the soy sauce,
sesame oil, olive oil, lemon juice and
honey and pour the dressing over the
noodles. Add the tomatoes, cucumber,
red pepper, coriander or basil, if using,
and spring onions, then toss well.
3 Heat a griddle pan or grill. Arrange
the strips of tuna in the pan, pour over
half the teriyaki sauce and cook for 2
minutes or until the fish is done to
your liking, turning halfway and
cooking in batches if necessary.
4 Spoon the noodle salad into four
bowls and top with the strips of tuna.
Sprinkle with sesame seeds, if liked.

MARVELLOUS MEDITERRANEAN COD

This simple roasted cod and vegetable dish is served with a garlicky herb sauce but if your children aren't into herbs, garlic mayonnaise works equally well. A salad is all that is needed as an accompaniment.

Serves 4
600g/1lb 5oz small new potatoes
2 tbsp olive oil
8 shallots, peeled
12 cherry tomatoes
3 sprigs fresh oregano
4 thick cod fillets, skinned, about 600g/1lb 5oz total weight
1 lemon, sliced

for the herb sauce:
4 tbsp olive oil
1 garlic clove, crushed
4 tbsp chopped fresh parsley
2 tbsp chopped fresh mint
juice of ½ lemon
salt and pepper, to taste

1 Preheat the oven to 200°C/400°F. Wash the potatoes and place them in a large roasting dish (you may need to use two) and toss in the oil. Roast in the oven for 30–35 minutes, turning occasionally. After 15 minutes, add the shallots and stir to coat with oil. Return to the oven.

2 Add the tomatoes and oregano to the vegetables and arrange the cod fillets on top. Season with salt and pepper. Top the fish with the lemon slices and bake for a further 10 minutes or until the vegetables and potatoes are tender and cod is cooked.
3 Meanwhile, put all the ingredients for the herb sauce in a blender and process until combined.
4 To serve, remove the herbs and lemon slices from the fish and arrange the shallots and tomatoes on four plates. Top with the fish (children may prefer the fish cut into chunks) and accompany with the potatoes and herb sauce.

BRAIN BOX

Fresh fish is a low-fat, high-protein source of B-group vitamins, zinc, selenium, calcium, vital for healthy nerves and mental processing.

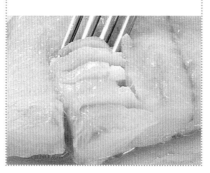

CREAMY LENTIL & HADDOCK CHOWDER

This comforting and sustaining thick soup is full of brain-stimulating goodness – make sure you buy the naturally undyed haddock, not the bright yellow variety. The soup makes a perfect weekend lunch served with crusty bread.

Serves 4
600g/1lb 5oz undyed smoked haddock fillets
milk, for poaching
200g/1 cup dried split red lentils
1 bay leaf
1 large leek, sliced
1 carrot, sliced
1 stick celery, sliced
750ml/3 cups vegetable stock
200g/1¼ cups canned 'no sugar or salt' sweetcorn, drained and rinsed
2 tbsp crème fraîche or single cream
salt and pepper, to taste
1 tsp chopped chives or parsley, to serve

1 Place the haddock in a large shallow pan and cover with milk. Poach for 8 minutes until cooked and opaque. Remove the fish from the pan, reserving the poaching liquid, and leave to cool. Remove the skin and any bones that may remain and flake the fish into large pieces. Set aside.
2 Place the lentils, bay leaf, leek, carrot, celery and stock in a large

BRAIN BOX

B-group vitamins found in **lentils and fish** help the body to release the energy from foods necessary for efficient brain function. They cannot be stored in the body (except B_{12}) so need to be replenished on a daily basis.

saucepan. Bring to the boil, skim off any foam that rises to the surface and reduce the heat. Simmer for 25–30 minutes, half-covered, until the lentils and vegetables are very tender, adding the corn 5 minutes before the end of the cooking time.

3 Remove the bay leaf and using a hand blender or food processor, purée the soup slightly so that some vegetable pieces remain. Add 125ml/ ½ cup of the poaching milk and the crème fraîche or cream, stir well and heat through. Gently mix in the haddock, making sure you don't break up the chunks, and season to taste. Spoon into bowls and top with chopped chives or parsley.

STIMULATING SALMON CAKES WITH PEA PURÉE

Vegetable purées can be a useful way of encouraging children to eat their greens – here, the creamy pea sauce is flavoured with mint. Fresh salmon is used but canned salmon makes a convenient alternative, albeit not as rich in omega-3 essential fatty acids.

Serves 4
350g/12oz skinless salmon fillets
milk, for poaching
650g/1lb 7oz potatoes, peeled and cut
  into chunks
1 tbsp tomato ketchup
2 tsp Dijon mustard
2 spring onions, thinly sliced
salt and pepper, to taste
flour, for dusting
sunflower oil, for frying

for the pea purée:
115g/1 cup frozen peas
2 tbsp single cream
2 tsp chopped fresh mint
salt and pepper, to taste

1 Put the salmon in a large shallow pan and just cover with milk. Bring to the boil, then reduce the heat and simmer for 3–4 minutes until just cooked. Remove the fish from the pan and reserve the milk. Leave the salmon to cool slightly then flake the flesh into large chunks, removing any bones.

2 Meanwhile, boil the potatoes for 15 minutes or until very tender. Drain and mash with 2–3 tablespoons of the reserved poaching milk – you want quite a dry yet lump-free mash.

3 Stir the ketchup, mustard, spring onions and half of the salmon into the mashed potato. Season to taste. Mix thoroughly until well combined, then add the rest of the salmon to the potato mixture, mixing gently to avoid breaking up the fish.

4 Pour some flour on to a large plate. Lightly dust your hands with flour and shape the mixture into eight cakes. Dip each one into flour to coat lightly. Place the fish cakes on a baking sheet, cover with clingfilm, and refrigerate for 30 minutes to firm up.

5 Heat enough oil to generously cover the base of a large frying pan. Cook the fish cakes, two or three at a time, for 3 minutes on each side until crisp and golden brown.

6 Meanwhile, cook the peas for 2 minutes. Drain well and transfer to a blender or food processor with the cream and mint. Purée then season to taste. Reheat if necessary and serve with the fish cakes.

PERFECT IN PINK

Trout is another member of the oily fish family and its pale pink flesh has a light texture and mild fishy flavour. Here, it is coated in a crispy oatmeal coating and briefly pan fried. You can usually find oatmeal in the breakfast cereal section in supermarkets. Serve the trout fillets with new potatoes and steamed vegetables.

Serves 4
4 x trout fillets, about 500g/1lb 2oz
    total weight
medium oatmeal, for coating
salt and pepper, to taste
1 small egg, beaten
large knob of butter
2 tbsp sunflower oil, for frying
lemon wedges, for squeezing

for the sauce:
4 tbsp dill sauce
2 tbsp mayonnaise

1 Skin the fish using a small sharp knife, then rinse the fillets and pat dry with kitchen towels. Cut each one into 2.5 cm/1 in wide strips.
2 Cover a plate with oatmeal and season it with salt and pepper. Dip each piece of fish in the beaten egg and then into the oatmeal, until covered on both sides.
3 Heat half the butter and oil in a large heavy-based frying pan. Add half of the trout strips and cook for 2 minutes on one side, turn over and cook for a further minute; keep warm. Add the remaining butter and oil to the pan and cook the remaining fish.
4 To make the sauce, mix together the dill sauce and mayonnaise. Divide the trout between four plates and serve with a spoonful of the sauce and a wedge of lemon for squeezing.

PERFECT PRAWN PASTA

This incredibly easy light pasta dish tastes special and is a perfect meal for the end of the day, when the pasta will help to calm the mind. Serve with a mixed salad.

Serves 4
250g/9oz wholewheat spaghetti
1 tbsp olive oil
1 large garlic clove, chopped
2 tsp dried oregano
60ml/¼ cup dry white wine
400ml/1⅔ cups passata
½ tsp sugar
2 heaped tbsp cream cheese
75g/¾ cup frozen peas, defrosted
175g/6oz cooked prawns, defrosted if
    frozen
salt and pepper, to taste

1 Cook the pasta in plenty of boiling salted water according to the packet instructions. Drain, reserving 2 tablespoons of the cooking water.

2 Meanwhile, heat the oil in a large heavy-based frying pan and cook the garlic and oregano for 1 minute until softened, taking care not to let the garlic burn. Add the wine and bring to the boil, then simmer over a medium-high heat until the liquid has reduced slightly and no smell of alcohol remains.
3 Stir in the passata and sugar, reduce the heat and simmer for 10 minutes until reduced and thickened. Stir in the cream cheese, peas and prawns and season to taste. Cook for a few minutes until heated through.
4 Combine the pasta and reserved cooking water with the sauce and serve immediately.

ROASTED RED PESTO CHICKEN

Chicken is an excellent source of low-fat protein but make sure you buy organic, free-range poultry for improved flavour and quality. This dish includes a recipe for red pesto but you can use a ready-made version, if preferred, but opt for a good quality one. Serve with roast potatoes and plenty of veg.

Serves 4
4 x skinless, boneless chicken breasts, about 600g/1lb 5oz total weight
1 tbsp olive oil
2 tbsp pine nuts

for the red pesto:
130g/4¾oz sun-blush tomatoes in oil (drained weight), chopped
2 garlic cloves, crushed
4 tbsp pine nuts
150ml/⅔ cup extra-virgin olive oil
55g/¾ cup freshly grated Parmesan

1 Preheat the oven to 200°C/400°F. To make the red pesto, put the ingredients in a food processor and blend until it forms a coarse purée.
2 Arrange the chicken in a large ovenproof dish. Brush each breast with the oil then spread a tablespoon of red pesto over each one until completely covered. Any leftover pesto can be stored in an airtight container in the fridge for up to a week.

3 Roast the chicken for 30 minutes or until the juices run clear when it is pierced with a skewer and there is no sign of any pink.
4 Meanwhile, lightly toast the pine nuts in a dry frying pan. Arrange the chicken breasts on four plates and sprinkle with the nuts and serve with roast potatoes and steamed vegetables.

BRAIN BOX

Selenium, zinc and B-group vitamins are found in **turkey**, all of which are essential to brain function. **Prawns** are also a good source of zinc, while the **peas** provide plentiful amounts of vitamin C and betacarotene.

PEACEFUL PAELLA

Experts have found that rice contains tryptophan which helps to boost the production of the calming chemical serotonin. Turkey has a similar effect, so a good night's sleep is on the cards!

Serves 4
2 tbsp olive oil
1 large onion, diced
2 x skinless, boneless turkey breasts, about 350g/12oz total weight, cut into bite-sized pieces
1 red pepper, seeded and diced
2 garlic cloves, chopped
2 tomatoes, seeded and chopped
1 tbsp tomato purée
pinch of saffron
800ml/3½ cups hot chicken or vegetable stock
250g/generous 1 cup paella rice
115g/1 cup frozen peas
150g/5½oz cooked prawns, defrosted if frozen
salt and pepper, to taste

1 Heat the oil in a large heavy-based lidded sauté pan. Add the onion and cook, covered, for 7 minutes until softened. Add the turkey, red pepper and garlic and cook for 5 minutes over a medium heat, stirring frequently, until the turkey is browned all over.
2 Add the tomato, tomato purée, saffron and stock to the pan. Stir in the rice and bring to the boil. Reduce the heat and simmer, covered, for 15 minutes or until the rice is tender.
3 Add the peas, prawns and seasoning and cook for a further 2 minutes, stirring frequently, until the prawns have heated through and the peas are cooked.

TIME-FOR-BED FRICASSÉE

This creamy yet low-fat dish features a healthy combination of turkey, vegetables and beans. Served with rice, it makes a balanced and brain-nourishing light supper. The white wine adds a rounded flavour to the dish and as the alcohol is cooked out, there are none of the negative affects – but you can leave it out if preferred and up the amount of stock accordingly.

Serves 4
1 tbsp plain flour
salt and pepper, to taste
4 x skinless turkey breasts, about 600g/1lb 5oz total weight, cut into bite-sized pieces
1 tbsp olive oil
1 large onion, finely chopped
2 garlic cloves, chopped
1 red pepper, seeded and diced
2 tsp dried oregano
2 carrots, finely diced
2 corn-on-the-cobs, kernels sliced off
60ml/¼ cup dry white wine
150ml/⅔ cup chicken or vegetable stock
4 tbsp half-fat crème fraîche
200g/¾ cup canned flageolet beans, drained and rinsed

1 Sprinkle the flour on a plate and season with salt and pepper. Toss the turkey pieces in the flour. Heat the oil in a large heavy-based lidded sauté pan over medium heat and fry the onion for 7 minutes. Remove the onion and add the turkey pieces. Brown for 10–15 minutes, turning the meat often to prevent it burning. Add a little stock to the pan if the meat begins to stick.
2 Return the onion to the pan with the garlic, pepper and oregano and cook for a further 2–3 minutes until the pepper has softened. Add the carrots, corn kernels and white wine then increase the heat and boil until the liquid has reduced and the alcohol has evaporated – any smell of wine should have disappeared.
3 Reduce the heat, add the stock and cook, covered, for 10 minutes. Stir in the crème fraîche and beans and warm through. Season to taste and serve.

PORK & APPLE PAN-FRY

Pork tenderloin is used here since it is lean and cooks quickly. The apple is perfect with pork and the beans add healthy low-fat protein and vital brain minerals. Serve with new potatoes or rice and salad.

Serves 4
1 tbsp plain flour
1 tsp paprika
700g/1lb 9oz pork tenderloin, trimmed and cut into bite-sized pieces
1½ tbsp olive oil
1 large onion, finely chopped
1 large dessert apple, cored, peeled and cut into bite-sized pieces
1 tbsp chopped fresh rosemary
300ml/1¼ cups vegetable stock
2 tomatoes, seeded and roughly chopped
400g/1½ cups can flageolet beans, drained and rinsed
2 tbsp half-fat crème fraîche
salt and pepper, to taste

> **BRAIN** BOX
>
> Make sure you use good quality lean **organic pork** for this recipe. Red meat is a good source of iron, a lack of which is common in children and has been linked to behavioural problems, including mood swings, irritability and hyperactivity.

1 Mix together the flour and paprika on a plate. Add the pork pieces and toss in the seasoned flour, shaking off any excess flour.

2 Heat the oil in a heavy-based frying pan over medium heat, add the pork and cook for 5 minutes, turning the meat until browned all over. Add the onion and cook for a further 7 minutes until softened. Mix in the apple and rosemary and cook for 3–4 minutes until the apples begin to break up.

3 Pour in the stock, bring to the boil, then reduce the heat and simmer for 15 minutes until reduced and thickened. Stir in the tomatoes and beans then cook for another 10 minutes over low heat. Stir in the crème fraîche and heat through before serving. Season to taste and serve.

COTTAGE PIE WITH A TWIST

I've used beef mince here but this mildly spiced cottage pie can be made with a vegetarian alternative if preferred. Add the veggie mince at step 4, with the spices. Steamed broccoli and sugar snap peas are perfect accompaniments.

Serves 4
1½ tbsp olive oil
1 onion, finely chopped
500g/1lb 2oz lean minced beef
1 carrot, grated
1 stick celery, finely chopped
2 garlic cloves, chopped
1 bay leaf
60ml/¼ cup dry white wine (optional)
1 tsp paprika
1 tsp ground cumin
1 tsp ground coriander
600ml/2½ cups passata
150ml/⅔ cup vegetable stock
200g/¾ cup canned cannellini beans, drained and rinsed
salt and pepper, to taste
2 tsp sesame seeds

for the sweet potato mash:
250g/9oz sweet potatoes, peeled and cut into chunks
450g/1lb potatoes, peeled and cut into chunks
25g/¼ stick butter
120ml/½ cup warm milk

1 Preheat the oven to 200°C/400°F. To make the sweet potato mash, cook both types of potato in boiling salted water for 15 minutes until tender. Drain and add the butter and warm milk. Mash until smooth and season to taste; set aside.

2 Meanwhile, heat the oil in a large heavy-based saucepan and cook the onion, covered, for 7 minutes until softened. Stir in the mince and cook, stirring frequently, until browned. Add the carrot, celery, garlic and bay leaf and cook, covered, for another 5 minutes, stirring frequently.

3 Add the wine, increase the heat and boil for 3 minutes until reduced and the alcohol has evaporated. Add the spices and cook for 1 minute, stirring frequently, then pour in the passata and stock. Bring to the boil, then reduce the heat and stir in the beans. Simmer, half-covered, for 10 minutes until reduced and thickened and season to taste.

4 Transfer the mince mixture to an ovenproof dish and spoon the mash over. Spread the mash with the back of a spoon until the mince is covered, then sprinkle the top with sesame seeds. Bake for 25–30 minutes until the mash starts to become crisp and brown on top.

SAUSAGE & BEAN HOTPOT

Good quality pork sausages are used in this warming, substantial stew but you could quite easily use vegetarian ones. Beans, vegetables and nuts are also included to provide a wide range of brain-boosting nutrients. Serve with a baked potato and a green vegetable.

Serves 4

8 good quality pork or vegetarian
   sausages
2 tbsp olive oil
1 large onion, finely chopped
2 garlic cloves, chopped
1 tsp dried thyme
1 tsp dried mixed herbs
1 red pepper, seeded and diced
675g/1lb 8oz butternut squash,
   seeded, peeled and cut into bite-
   sized pieces
185ml/¾ cup fresh apple juice
375ml/1½ cups vegetable or chicken
   stock
1 tsp Dijon mustard
200g/¾ cup canned cannellini beans,
   drained and rinsed
2 heaped tbsp unsalted, unroasted
   cashew nuts
60ml/¼ cup milk
1 slice wholemeal bread, crusts
   removed and broken into pieces
salt and pepper, to taste

BRAIN BOX

Butternut squash contain antioxidants betacarotene, lycopene and vitamin C, which help to promote mental alertness and memory by protecting nerve cells in the brain. Red peppers have similar properties.

1 Preheat the grill to medium-high and line a grill pan with foil. Grill the sausages, turning occasionally, until browned and cooked through. Set aside.

2 Meanwhile, heat the oil in a large saucepan over medium heat. Add the onion and fry, covered, for 7 minutes, stirring occasionally, until softened. Add the garlic, herbs and red pepper and cook, covered, for a further 3 minutes. Stir in the butternut squash, stir well and cook for 5 minutes.

3 Pour in the apple juice. Increase the heat and bring to the boil and cook for 3 minutes until the juice has reduced. Lower the heat to medium, pour in the stock and stir in the mustard and beans then cook, uncovered, for 15 minutes.

4 While the hotpot is cooking, grind the nuts in a food processor, then add the milk and bread. Continue to process to make a thick paste. Stir the paste into the hotpot – this will help to thicken the stock. Cook for another 5 minutes until thickened and season to taste before serving.

BRAIN BOX

Lean organic beef can play a part in a healthy diet if eaten in moderation. Meat is a complete protein and a good source of iron, zinc and some B-group vitamins in a readily absorbable form. A lack of iron has been linked to learning difficulties and poor concentration. Organic beef is free from the cocktail of chemicals such as hormones and growth promoters that intensively reared animals are often exposed to.

AUTUMN BEEFY BRAINY STEW

It is important to use good quality organic beef for this hearty stew. Don't be put off by the length of time it takes to cook since it doesn't require any lengthy involvement from the cook and the slow-cooking results in a rich, thick gravy and succulent meat. Serve with mash and a green vegetable.

Serves 4

3 tbsp flour
salt and pepper, to taste
750g/1lb 10oz lean diced organic
    casserole beef
3 tbsp olive oil
12 shallots, peeled and halved or
    quartered if large
2 carrots, cut into batons
1 parsnip, sliced into rounds
2 bay leaves
1 tbsp chopped fresh rosemary
1 tbsp chopped fresh thyme
450ml/1¾ cups brown ale
250ml/1 cup beef stock
1 tbsp Worcestershire sauce
200g/7oz canned
    chestnuts, drained

1 Preheat the oven to 170°C/325°F. Put the flour in a clean plastic food bag or on a plate and season generously. Toss the beef in the seasoned flour until coated. Heat 1 tbsp oil in a large flameproof, ovenproof casserole dish. Add one-third of the beef and cook for 5–6 minutes, turning occasionally, until browned all over – the meat may stick to the pan until it is properly sealed. Remove the browned beef from the pan and cook the remaining two batches, adding another 1 tbsp oil when necessary. Set aside when all the beef has been sealed.

2 Add the remaining oil to the pan with the shallots, carrots, parsnip and herbs and cook for 3 minutes, stirring occasionally.

3 Pour in the ale and bring to the boil. Cook over a high heat until the alcohol in the ale has evaporated and the liquid has reduced. Add the stock and Worcestershire sauce then cook for another 3 minutes.

4 Stir in the chestnuts and beef. Make sure the liquid returns to the boil, then cover the dish and transfer to the oven. Cook for 2 hours until the stock has formed a rich gravy and the meat is tender. Season to taste before serving.

PICNICS AND PARTIES

Finding a good range of nutritious picnic and party food can be quite a challenge, but this section contains a selection of innovative and fun sweet and savoury recipes that won't fail to appeal to everyone.

MAGIC FAIRY BOWL

If your kids need extra encouragement to eat fruit, this pretty party piece may be just the thing. The hollowed out melon is filled with your chosen fruit to give a stunning result.

Serves 6
½ large Charentais or cantaloupe melon, seeds scooped out
a selection of fruits, such as strawberries, raspberries, slices of nectarine or peach, orange segments or seedless grapes

1 Cut a sliver off the base of the melon so it stands up and place on a serving plate. Scoop out most of the flesh using a melon baller or teaspoon to leave a hollow bowl shape, setting the fruit aside.
2 Fill the melon half with the fruit of your choice mixed with the melon balls, pouring over any juice.

BRAIN BOX

Melons, particularly the orange-fleshed variety, contain useful amounts of the brain-protecting antioxidants betacarotene and vitamin C as well as folic acid and vitamin B_6.

MELON BOATS

Fun and healthy too, these melon sailing boats are a simple idea but make a great addition to any party tea. Choose natural cheese slices to avoid unwanted additives. Take care when offering these boats to very small children because of the cocktail sticks.

Makes 12 boats
1 small melon, such as galia, Charentais or cantaloupe
12 natural cheese slices, like Gruyère, Edam or Cheddar
12 cocktail sticks

1 Cut the melon in half and scoop out the seeds. Cut each half into 6 wedges.
2 Thread each cheese slice on to a cocktail stick so that the slices look like sails and the sticks are the masts. You could stick a paper flag on the top of each stick.
3 Stick each cheese sail into a melon wedge to make the boats and serve.

HALLOUMI, HAM & PINEAPPLE STICKS

Children love this nifty twist on the traditional cheesy pineapple but take care when serving them to young children. If possible, use fresh instead of canned pineapple, since it is richer in vitamins that are lost in the canning process. Cherry tomatoes, bacon and nectarine slices make tasty alternatives.

BRAIN BOX

Pineapple contains manganese which aids poor memory by improving oxygenation and protecting brain tissue.

Makes 12 sticks
250g/9oz halloumi cheese, cut into 24 cubes
1 small pineapple, peeled
2 thick slices good quality lean ham, cut into 24 cubes

1 Preheat the grill to high and line the grill pan with foil. Arrange the cubes of halloumi in the pan and grill lightly, turning occasionally, until just golden. Leave to cool slightly.
2 Cut the pineapple into thick slices, remove the core and cut into 24 chunks.
3 Thread a chunk of pineapple on to a cocktail stick, followed by a cube of halloumi. Place a cube of ham on to the stick and then a final chunk of pineapple. Repeat to make 12 sticks.

PIZZA PRESTO!

By making your own pizzas you can avoid the unwanted additives often included in over-processed shop-bought versions. This pizza is perfect when time is short since the base doesn't require prolonged kneading and rising.

Makes 8
55g/½ cup wholemeal self-raising flour
175g/1½ cups self-raising flour
2 tsp dried oregano
1 tsp salt
4 tbsp olive oil

for the topping:
1 tbsp olive oil
1 garlic clove, crushed
300ml/1¼ cups passata
2 tsp sun-dried tomato paste
8 slices mozzarella
2 tbsp grated Cheddar cheese

1 To make the pizza bases, combine the two different types of flour, oregano and salt in a mixing bowl. Add half of the olive oil and 150ml water. Mix with your hands to make a soft dough.
2 Turn out the dough on to a lightly floured work surface. Knead until it forms a smooth dough then wrap in cling film and allow to rest while you make the tomato sauce.

3 To make the topping, heat the olive oil in a medium-sized heavy-based saucepan over medium-low heat. Fry the garlic for 1 minute then add the passata and tomato paste and cook for 8 minutes, stirring occasionally, until reduced and thickened.
4 Meanwhile, divide the dough into 8 pieces and roll out each piece into a round, about 6 cm/2½ in in diameter. Heat half the remaining oil in a large heavy-based frying pan. Arrange half of the pizza bases in the pan and cook for 2–3 minutes on each side until golden. Keep warm while you cook the remaining pizza bases, adding the rest of the oil if necessary.
5 Preheat the grill to medium-high. Spread the tomato sauce over the bases and top each one with a slice of mozzarella and a sprinkling of Cheddar. Grill for 1–2 minutes until the mozzarella has melted and is beginning to turn golden.

BRAIN BOX

B-group vitamins provided by **eggs and ham** help feed the brain to improve mental clarity and motivation.

PICNIC PIES

There's no high-fat pastry in these pies, instead a slice of good-quality lean ham is used as a base for the quiche-style filling. They are just as delicious cold as warm and are the right size for children to hold.

Makes 8
butter, for greasing
8 small slices lean good-quality ham
3 eggs, beaten
240ml/scant 1 cup milk
50g/scant ½ cup grated mature
   Cheddar cheese
pepper
2 tomatoes, sliced

1 Preheat the oven to 180°C/350°F. Lightly grease an 8-hole deep muffin tin with some butter. Line the base and sides of each hole with a slice of ham, folding the ham where necessary, to make cup shapes.
2 Mix together the eggs, milk and cheese, season with a little pepper, and pour the mixture into each ham-lined muffin hole. Top each one with a slice of tomato and bake for 15–20 minutes until the egg filling has risen and set. Leave to cool slightly then transfer to a wire rack to cool further. Serve warm or cold.

TUNA & LEEK FRITTATA

Transported whole or cut into chunky wedges, a frittata makes a protein-rich nutritious addition to a picnic or packed lunch box that will fight hunger pangs and provide plenty of brain energy for the rest of the day.

Serves 4–6
1 tbsp olive oil
small knob of butter
1 large leek, finely sliced
200g/7oz can tuna in olive oil or spring
    water, drained
6 eggs, beaten
salt and pepper, to taste

1 Heat the oil and butter in a medium-sized, ovenproof frying pan then fry the leek for 5–7 minutes until softened. Stir in the tuna, making sure that there is an even distribution of leek and tuna and that some chunks of tuna remain.
2 Preheat the grill to medium-high. Season the beaten eggs and pour them carefully over the tuna and leek mixture. Cook over a moderate heat for 5 minutes or until the eggs are just set and the base of the frittata is golden brown.
3 Place the pan under the grill and cook the top of the frittata for 3 minutes or until set and lightly golden. Serve the frittata warm or cold, cut into wedges or fingers.

HAPPY CHICKEN STICKS

Chicken is a high quality, low fat – as long as the skin has been removed – protein, but make sure you buy organic, free-range meat to avoid added chemicals. Try these dipped into satay sauce (see page 70).

Makes 16
4 skinless, boneless chicken breasts,
    about 450g/1lb total weight
2 tbsp olive oil
juice of ½ lemon
salt and pepper, to taste

1 Soak 16 wooden skewers in a bowl of water for 30 minutes to prevent them burning. Cut each chicken breast lengthways into four strips and thread each one on to a skewer.
2 Combine the olive oil, lemon juice and seasoning in a small bowl then brush the chicken with the mixture.
3 Heat a griddle pan or grill to medium-hot. Cook the chicken skewers for 3 minutes on each side until golden and cooked through, making sure there is no trace of pink inside. Cook for slightly longer if there is any sign of pinkness.

FIRED-UP FALAFEL

Beans, with the exception of the baked variety, are often neglected in children's diets but they offer a beneficial range of vital minerals for the brain. Serve these falafel in mini sesame-seed-coated pitta breads along with some humous and the salad leaves of your choice – yum!

Makes 12 falafel

400g/14oz can chickpeas, drained and
   rinsed
2 cloves garlic, crushed
2 spring onions, finely sliced
1 tsp ground cumin
1 tsp ground coriander
1 tbsp sesame seeds
1 egg, beaten
flour, for dusting
sunflower oil, for frying
mini sesame-seed pitta breads, red
   pepper humous (see page 59) and
   salad leaves, to serve

1 Put the chickpeas, garlic, spring onions, cumin, coriander and sesame seeds in a food processor and blend until the beans are roughly chopped. Add the egg and blend again until the mixture forms a coarse paste. Place in the refrigerator for 1 hour to allow the mixture to firm up.
2 Form the mixture into 12 walnut-sized balls using lightly floured hands then roll in flour until lightly coated.

BRAIN BOX

Beans are a useful blend of protein and carbohydrate and are low in fat to boot. These nutrients work in tandem to build the brain's neurotransmitters and provide long-term energy.

3 Heat 1 tablespoon of oil in a large heavy-based frying pan and cook the falafel in batches (adding more oil if necessary) for 6 minutes, turning occasionally, until golden. Drain on kitchen towels.
4 Warm each pitta bread and split along one side. Spread the inside with humous and place two falafel in each one (you could cut them in half if easier to handle). Add the salad leaves of your choice and serve.

BETTER-FOR-YOU BABY BURGERS

By using good quality, preferably organic, ingredients, you can have a healthy and delicious burger in next to no time.

Makes 10 burgers

40g/¾ cup fresh wholemeal
   breadcrumbs
1 tsp dried oregano
1 onion, grated
1 carrot, finely grated

1 garlic clove, crushed
450g/1lb lean minced beef or
  vegetarian alternative
1 egg, beaten
salt and pepper, to taste
flour, for dusting
sunflower oil, for frying
10 mini burger buns, to serve
sliced tomato and lettuce leaves, to
  serve
mayonnaise, relish or tomato ketchup,
  to serve, if liked

1 Place the breadcrumbs, oregano, onion, carrot, garlic, mince and egg in a large bowl. Season and mix with your hands until all the ingredients are combined. Shape the mixture into 10 smallish balls using floured hands. Set aside in the refrigerator for 15 minutes.
2 Heat enough oil to lightly cover the base of a large heavy-based frying pan. Place the balls in the hot oil, flattening each one with a spatula, and fry in batches for 3 minutes on each side until browned and cooked through.
3 Split the burger buns in half and add the burgers. Serve with sliced tomato, lettuce and the accompaniment of your choice.

PICNIC FOCACCIA

There's something very satisfying about making bread and children love to get involved in the kneading and shaping.

Serves 6–8
250g/2¼ cups strong wholemeal flour
250g/2¼ cups strong white flour, plus
  extra for dusting
7g/⅛oz sachet instant dried yeast
2 tsp salt
350ml/1⅓ cups lukewarm water
200g/7oz mozzarella cheese, sliced
handful fresh basil leaves
8 sun-blush tomatoes, roughly sliced
1 tsp oil from the sun-blush tomatoes
  or extra-virgin olive oil
2 tsp extra-virgin olive oil
coarse sea salt, for sprinkling (optional)

1 Combine both types of flour with the yeast and salt in a large mixing bowl. Make a well in the centre and pour in the water. Stir initially with a wooden spoon and then with your hands. Knead to make a soft, slightly sticky dough, adding a little more water or flour if the dough is too dry or wet.
2 Turn out the dough on a lightly floured work surface. Knead for 15 minutes – push the dough flat with the palm of your hand then fold the far edge towards you, giving it a half turn, then repeat the process. Place the dough in the cleaned bowl, cover with a tea towel and leave it to rest somewhere warm and out of a draught for 45–60 minutes until doubled in size.
3 Divide the dough into two pieces. Roll out each piece to fit a 22 cm/8½ in round baking tin. Press one half into the lightly floured tin. Top with the cheese, basil leaves and tomatoes. Sprinkle the oil from the tomatoes over the top.
4 Place the other half of dough on top, pressing down the edges firmly over the filling to seal. Cover the focaccia with a tea towel and set aside for another 30 minutes to rise. Preheat the oven to 220°C/425°F.
5 Make indentations in the bread with your fingers, sprinkle the olive oil over the top and the coarse sea salt, if using. Bake for 35 minutes until risen and golden. Remove from the tin and tap the base of the bread with your fingers – it should sound hollow when cooked through. Leave to cool on a wire rack.

BRAIN BOX

Protein supplied by the **cheese** and carbohydrates in the **flour** work together to keep blood-glucose levels steady and consequently help to avoid dips in concentration and mental alertness.

SUPER SEEDY BREADSTICKS

Children will love making these breadsticks, which make healthy energy-boosting snacks eaten on their own or dipped into humous or similar alternative. Store in an airtight container for a couple of days or freeze for later use.

Makes about 55 breadsticks
4 tbsp sunflower seeds
3 tbsp olive oil
250g/2¼ cups strong white flour, plus extra for dusting
250g/2¼ cups strong wholemeal flour
7g/⅛ oz sachet instant dried yeast
1½ tsp salt
300ml/1¼ cups lukewarm water
1 egg, beaten
1 tbsp milk
sesame seeds, for sprinkling

1 Lightly toast the sunflower seeds in a dry frying pan. Transfer to a food processor with 1 tablespoon of the olive oil and grind to make a rough paste. Set aside to cool.
2 Combine both types of flour with the yeast and salt. Add the ground seeds, water and the rest of the oil, mixing initially with a wooden spoon and then your hands to make a soft, slightly sticky dough, adding more water or flour if the dough seems too dry or wet.

3 Dust the work surface with flour and knead the dough for 10 minutes – push it flat with the palm of your hand, then fold the far edge towards you, giving it a half turn, then repeat the process. Place the dough in a clean bowl, cover with a tea towel and leave it to rest somewhere warm and out of a draught for 10 minutes.
4 Preheat the oven to 220°C/425°F. Roll out the dough into a very thin rectangle, halve the dough horizontally and cut into 1 cm/½ in wide strips. Roll each piece of dough into a sausage-shape using both hands and

BRAIN BOX

Calcium, zinc, magnesium, potassium, vitamin E and omega-6 essential fatty acids (EFAs) are found in beneficial amounts in **sunflower seeds**. EFAs are crucial for healthy brain development and have to be supplied by diet since the body is not able to make them itself.

place on a lightly floured baking sheet. You will probably need about 3 baking sheets as this dough makes about 55 breadsticks. Cover each sheet with a clean tea towel and set aside for 15 minutes until risen.
5 Mix together the beaten egg and milk and brush over each breadstick. Sprinkle each one with sesame seeds and bake for 15 minutes until crisp and golden. Transfer to a wire rack to cool.

FRUITY SODA BREAD

Soda bread is the perfect introduction to bread-making for children – it doesn't require lengthy kneading or rising as it doesn't contain yeast. Although dried fruit is high in natural sugars, it does provide valuable minerals which work synergistically to boost mental performance.

Serves 6–8
225g/2 cups strong white flour, plus extra for dusting
225g/2 cups strong wholemeal flour
1½ tsp salt
1 tsp bicarbonate of soda
1 heaped tbsp caster sugar
125g/1 cup ready-to-eat stoned prunes or dates, roughly chopped
1 egg, lightly beaten
300ml/1¼ cups buttermilk
2–3 tbsp natural live yogurt or milk (optional)

1 Preheat the oven to 200°C/400°F. Sift together both types of flour with the salt and bicarbonate of soda into a large bowl, adding any bran left in the sieve. Add the sugar and prunes and mix well to combine.

2 Make a well in the centre and add the beaten egg and buttermilk then mix initially with a wooden spoon and then your hands to form a soft, slightly sticky dough. If the dough is too dry, add the yogurt or milk.

3 Turn out the dough on a lightly floured work surface and knead lightly until the dough is smooth. Form into a flat round, about 4 cm/1½ in thick.

4 Place the loaf on a floured baking sheet and dust with flour. Cut a large deep cross in the dough then bake for 30–35 minutes until risen and golden – the bread should sound hollow when tapped on the bottom with your fingers. Transfer to a wire rack to cool.

BRAIN BOX

Wholemeal flour is richer in B-group vitamins, fibre, vitamin E, selenium and magnesium than its refined white counterpart. A lack of B-group vitamins can affect mental judgement and increase anxiety.

PARTY PEOPLE

These mini 'people-shaped' cheese scones make a fun addition to a party spread without containing heaps of sugar. Spread with cream cheese for a protein boost.

Makes 12 people
120g/1 cup plain flour, plus extra for dusting
120g/1 cup wholemeal flour
2 tsp baking powder
large pinch of salt
50g/½ stick chilled butter, cubed
3 tbsp freshly grated Parmesan cheese
1 egg, beaten
100ml/scant ½ cup milk, plus extra for glazing

1 Preheat the oven to 220°C/425°F and lightly grease 2 baking sheets. Sift both types of flour with the baking powder into a large bowl, and mix in the salt.

2 Rub in the butter with your fingertips until the mixture forms coarse breadcrumbs. Stir in the cheese. Make a well in the centre of the mixture and pour in the egg and milk. Mix initially with a wooden spoon and then with your hands to make a soft dough.

3 Turn out the dough on a lightly floured work surface and gently press into a round about 2.5 cm/1 in thick. Stamp out 12 scones using a small gingerbread man/woman cutter. Place on the prepared baking sheets, brush the tops with milk, and bake for 15 minutes until risen and golden. Transfer to a wire rack to cool.

MEGA-PASSION CAKE

This recipe makes a sizeable double-layered birthday cake but the recipe can be halved for an everyday tea cake. What's more, your children will never guess that this light, moist cake contains healthy carrots!

Serves 20
butter, for greasing
450g/4 cups self-raising flour
2 pinches of salt
2 tsp ground cinnamon
2 tsp ground nutmeg
450g/2 cups light muscovado sugar
450g/1lb carrots, grated
6 eggs, beaten
350ml/scant 1½ cups sunflower oil

for the icing:
160g/scant ¾ cup cream cheese
75g/¾ stick unsalted butter
1 tsp natural vanilla extract
80g/¾ cup unrefined icing sugar

to decorate:
low-sugar, natural-fruit jelly sweets, chocolate hundreds and thousands, candles

1 Preheat the oven to 180°C/350°F. Lightly grease two 20 cm/8 in square cake tins with butter and line the bases with baking parchment.
2 Sift the flour, salt and spices into a large mixing bowl. Add the sugar and carrots and mix well.

3 Mix together the eggs and oil then add to the mixture in the bowl, stirring with a wooden spoon until combined.
4 Pour the mixture into the prepared cake tins, level with the back of a spoon and bake for 50 minutes or until a skewer inserted into the centre of each cake comes out clean. Leave for 10 minutes, then carefully turn out the cakes to cool on wire racks.
5 To make the icing, beat together the cream cheese, butter and vanilla extract until light and creamy. Beat in the icing sugar, then place in the refrigerator for 15 minutes to harden slightly.
6 Level off the top of each cake with a knife then spread the icing over one cake. Place the second cake on top and spread with a final layer of icing – it doesn't matter if the icing runs down the sides. Decorate with the jelly sweets and sprinkle with chocolate hundreds and thousands. Candles add the finishing touch for a birthday or other celebration.

VARIATION
Swap the carrots for 6 mashed ripe bananas; the combination of bananas and nutmeg are said to encourage restful sleep.

CLEVER-BUT-NUTTY COLESLAW

This is nothing like commercially made coleslaws where the artificial-tasting vegetables are dripping in dressing with a smattering of the usual preservatives and other additives. For the optimum amount of nutrients and best flavour, prepare this version as close to serving as possible.

BRAIN BOX

Cabbage and carrots are rich in antioxidants and help to protect the brain from damaging toxins.

Pumpkin seeds are one of the few foods to contain both omega-3 and omega-6 essential fatty acids.

Walnuts and olive oil further boost the essential fatty acid content, which are vital for an efficient nervous system and healthy brain cells.

Serves 6
110g/2 cups finely shredded white cabbage
2 carrots, grated
2 spring onions, finely sliced on the diagonal
1 tbsp chopped walnuts (or other nuts of your choice)
2 tbsp pumpkin or sunflower seeds
1 dessert apple, cored and diced

for the dressing:
2 tbsp extra-virgin olive oil
1 tbsp fresh lemon juice, plus extra for coating
4 tbsp mayonnaise

1 Mix together the cabbage, carrots and spring onions in a salad bowl. Lightly toast the nuts and seeds in a dry frying pan for 2 minutes. Leave to cool. Stir the cooled nuts and seeds into the salad.
2 Mix together the ingredients for the dressing and pour it over the salad. Toss well to coat. Toss the apple pieces in the extra lemon juice to prevent it browning and sprinkle the apple over the top of the salad before serving.

BRAIN BOX

Couscous as a carbohydrate has a soothing, calming effect on the brain. Similarly, **basil**, which is found in the pesto, is a calming and mood-enhancing herb.

The protein in the **halloumi**, however will help to stimulate and enliven the mind.

CALMING COUSCOUS

Great for a packed lunch or picnic salad, couscous doesn't go soggy and lose flavour if left for a few hours.

Serves 4
125g/scant 2 cups couscous
2–3 tbsp green or red pesto, to taste
2 tsp olive oil
10 cherry tomatoes, halved
60g/½ cup cubed halloumi

1 Preheat the grill to medium and line the grill pan with foil. Put the couscous into a bowl, then pour over boiling water to cover by 5 mm/¼ in. Stir, then set aside until the water has been absorbed by the couscous. Fluff up with a fork and taste – if the couscous is still hard add a little more boiling water and leave for a few minutes more.
2 Arrange the halloumi in the grill pan and grill for a few minutes, turning occasionally, until golden on all sides.

3 Stir the pesto and oil into the couscous until it is thoroughly coated. Mix in the tomatoes and grilled halloumi and serve.

CARAMEL SESAME POPTASTIC

Good fun and incredibly easy to cook, popcorn is a party must. Additionally, this version is much lower in sugar than shop-bought popcorn and is also free of additives.

Serves 6–8
sunflower oil
90g/½ cup popcorn maize
25g/¼ stick unsalted butter
3 tbsp maple syrup
2 tbsp sesame seeds

1 Heat enough oil (about 1 tablespoon) to cover the bottom of a medium-sized heavy-based saucepan. When hot, add the popcorn in a single layer and cover with the lid. Cook over a medium heat, shaking the pan frequently, until the corn has popped. Do not lift the lid until the corn has finished popping. Transfer the popcorn to a large bowl.

2 Melt the butter in the pan and add the maple syrup. Bring to the boil then reduce the heat and simmer briefly until thickened. Leave to cool slightly then pour the buttery maple syrup over the popcorn and add the sesame seeds. Toss well to thoroughly coat the popcorn in the mixture. Leave to cool before serving.

BRAIN BOX

Corn is one of the most nutritionally balanced carbohydrates and as such is a good food for the brain and nervous system.

FEEL-GOOD BROWNIES

Chocolate boosts endorphin and serotonin levels in the brain, having an uplifting effect and encouraging a buoyant mood. That said, it should be eaten in moderation since chocolate also contains the stimulants caffeine and theobromine.

Makes 16 brownies
200g/2 sticks unsalted butter, plus extra for greasing
200g/7oz good quality plain chocolate (at least 75 per cent cocoa solids)
100g/¾ cup roughly chopped hazelnuts
3 eggs, beaten
225g/1 cup unrefined caster sugar
175g/1½ cups plain flour
1 tsp baking powder
65g/½ cup chopped ready-to-eat dates

1 Preheat the oven to 180°C/350°F. Grease a 30 x 20 cm/12 x 8 in baking tin with the extra butter and line with baking parchment.
2 Break the chocolate and place it with the butter in a heatproof bowl. Place the bowl over a pan of barely simmering water and heat until the chocolate and butter have melted, stirring once or twice. Set aside to cool slightly.
3 Meanwhile, lightly toast the hazelnuts in a dry frying pan until beginning to turn golden brown. Set aside to cool.

BRAIN BOX

These brownies are given a health boost thanks to the **hazelnuts and dates**. Hazelnuts contain a brain-stimulating combination of boron, B-group vitamins, iron, magnesium, selenium, zinc and omega-6 essential fatty acids. Many of these nutrients are boosted by the dates, particularly iron, magnesium, boron and B-group vitamins, which work together to ensure healthy brain function.

4 Whisk together the eggs and sugar in a large mixing bowl until light and fluffy. Then stir in the chocolate and butter mixture.
5 Sift half of the flour and all the baking powder into the chocolate mixture and fold in with a wooden spoon. Sift in the remaining flour and fold in. Carefully stir in the dates and hazelnuts until evenly distributed.
6 Pour the mixture into the prepared tin and bake for 25 minutes until the brownies have risen but are still soft in the centre. Leave to cool for 15 minutes before removing from the tin. Cut into 16 squares.

REAL FRUIT LOLLIES

Lower in sugar than most commercially made ice lollies – and certainly free from artificial colourings and other E-numbers – these home-made lollies are made from a real fresh fruit purée and fresh custard.

Makes 6 lollies
6 plums, halved and stoned
3 nectarines, stoned and roughly chopped
1–2 tbsp unrefined caster sugar, to taste
150ml/⅔ cup fresh custard

1 Put the plums and nectarines in a medium-sized, non-metallic saucepan. Add the sugar and 2 tbsp water. Bring to the boil, then reduce the heat and simmer for 5 minutes until softened. Taste for sweetness and add more sugar if too sour. Leave to cool then purée until smooth – you need about 250ml/1 cup of fruit purée.
2 Combine the fruit purée and custard then spoon the mixture into 6 ice-lolly moulds. Freeze until solid.

VARIATION
Orange and mango make a refreshing alternative. Juice the fruit in a juicer – you need about 400ml/1⅔ cups to make 6 lollies. Slice 1 orange into rounds and place a round into each ice-lolly mould then fill with the fruit juice. Freeze until solid.

Ice cream contains calcium which is needed for healthy nerve function and works in tandem with magnesium to reduce irritability and insomnia.

Strawberries and oranges are rich in the potent antioxidant vitamin C, which also helps to balance the brain's neurotransmitters, having an uplifting effect.

FRUITY-BOCKER GLORY

You can't go wrong with an ice cream sundae: this firm kids' favourite is a breeze to make and has been adapted to ensure a healthy twist.

Serves 4
250g/9oz strawberries, halved
2 tbsp fresh orange juice
1 tbsp unrefined caster sugar
1 tbsp flaked almonds or chopped nuts
8 scoops good quality vanilla ice cream
chocolate shavings, to serve

1 Put the strawberries and orange juice in a food processor or blender and purée until smooth. Sieve the mixture into a saucepan, to remove any seeds. Stir in the sugar and place the pan over a medium-low heat; cook for 5 minutes until the sauce thickens. Taste for sweetness and add more sugar if necessary; leave to cool.

2 Lightly toast the flaked almonds or chopped nuts in a dry frying pan. Set aside to cool.

3 To serve, place a few spoonfuls of sauce in a tall glass. Top with a scoop of ice cream and another spoonful of sauce. Add a final scoop of ice cream. Sprinkle the nuts over the top, then a few shavings of chocolate. Repeat to make four sundaes.

SWEET THINGS

All children love sweets and puddings but it's important that they get the right sort of desserts, rather than the highly sugary, additive-laden ones commonly available. Here you'll find a variety of puddings with a healthy twist, guaranteed to appeal to your child's taste buds.

PANCAKES WITH BAKED BANANAS

A favourite with children, these substantial pancakes make an energising family breakfast. Wholemeal flour will result in a denser pancake, for a lighter batter use half wholemeal and half white flour.

Serves 4
145g/1¼ cups wholemeal flour
pinch of salt
2 tbsp porridge oats
2 tbsp unrefined caster sugar
1 tsp baking powder
1 egg, beaten
284ml/1¼ cups buttermilk
150ml/⅔ cup milk
25g/¼ stick butter, melted
sunflower oil, for frying

for the baked bananas:
2 bananas
2 tbsp maple syrup

1 To make the baked bananas; preheat the oven to 180°C/350°F. Place the bananas on a baking sheet

BRAIN BOX

Bananas are energising foods and are a good source of the mineral potassium, which plays a key role in nerve cell function.

BRAIN BOX

Children are susceptible to the effects of fluctuating blood-sugar levels, which naturally fall overnight. **Whole grains** release their energy slowly in the body, ensuring blood-sugar levels are kept steady.

and bake for 20 minutes until tender. Leave to cool slightly before slicing.
2 Meanwhile, make the pancakes. Mix together the flour, salt, oats, caster sugar and baking powder.
3 Whisk together the egg, buttermilk, milk and melted butter, then add to the flour mixture. Beat well to remove any lumps, making a thick batter.
4 Lightly oil a large heavy-based frying pan. Place 2 tablespoons of batter per pancake in the hot oil – you will probably be able to cook 3 pancakes at a time. Cook each pancake for 3 minutes until the base is golden, then turn over and cook for a further 2 minutes. Place on a plate, covered with foil, to keep warm while you make the remaining pancakes.
5 To serve, divide the pancakes between four plates, spoon over the sliced baked bananas and drizzle with maple syrup.

FRUITY SHERBET

This refreshing ice is made from an antioxidant-rich combination of mangoes and oranges. It's simple to make and helps boost the recommended daily fruit intake.

Serves 6–8
120g/½ cup unrefined caster sugar
300ml/1¼ cups water
2 large mangoes, peeled, stoned and roughly chopped
juice of 3 oranges
1 egg white

1 Put the sugar and water in a saucepan and stir until the sugar is dissolved. Place over medium-high heat and bring to the boil, then reduce the heat and simmer for 5 minutes. Leave to cool.
2 Combine the mango, orange juice and sugar syrup in a food processor or blender and process until the fruit is puréed.
3 Pour the mixture into a freezer-proof container and freeze for 2 hours until semi-frozen. Remove from the freezer and break up any ice crystals using a hand whisk.
4 Whisk the egg white until it forms stiff peaks then fold into the semi-frozen mixture. Return to the freezer and freeze until solid.
5 Transfer the sherbet to the fridge to soften 30 minutes before serving.

BROWN BREAD ICE CREAM

Brown bread and ice cream may sound a strange combination but it is delicious and provides plentiful amounts of mind-stimulating energy.

Serves 6–8
130g/2 cups wholemeal breadcrumbs
115g/scant ½ cup demerara sugar
400ml/1⅔ cups whipping cream
2 eggs, separated
2 tbsp maple syrup

1 Preheat the oven to 160°C/325°F. Combine the breadcrumbs and sugar in a bowl then spread over a baking sheet. Bake, turning occasionally, until the crumbs are a dark golden colour (be careful not to burn them) and the sugar has almost dissolved – the mixture almost caramelizes. Set aside.
2 In a bowl, whip the cream to soft peaks. In a separate bowl, whisk the eggs whites until they form stiff peaks. Beat together the egg yolks and maple syrup in another bowl.
3 Stir the cooled sugary breadcrumbs and maple syrup mixture into the whipped cream then carefully fold in the egg whites. Spoon into a freezer-proof container and freeze for a few hours until firm. Leave to soften in the fridge for 20 minutes before serving.

BANANA ICE

Simple puddings are often the best and this couldn't be simpler. It's healthy as well, of course.

Serves 4
4 bananas, peeled
natural live bio yogurt, maple syrup and nuts, to serve (optional)

1 Wrap the bananas in clingfilm and place in the freezer. Freeze until solid, then remove the clingfilm and process in a blender until roughly chopped. The banana ice is delicious served on its own or can be topped with a spoonful of yogurt, a drizzle of maple syrup and a sprinkling of lightly toasted nuts.

STRAWBERRY & VANILLA YOGURT ICE

Lower in fat than cream-based ices, yogurt produces a more tangy, but no less delicious, dessert. Live natural bio yogurt is particularly good for the health of the digestive system, which is vital for the efficient absorption of nutrients from food.

Serves 6–8
450g/1lb strawberries, halved if large
450g/1lb Greek bio yogurt
4 tbsp icing sugar
1 tsp natural vanilla extract

1 Preheat the oven to 200°C/400°F. Grease a 12-hole muffin tin with the extra butter or line with muffin papers.
2 Mix together both types of flour with the sugar, baking powder and salt in a mixing bowl.
3 Beat the buttermilk, eggs and melted butter together in a separate bowl. Add the mixture to the dry ingredients and stir until combined – there may be a few lumps but this is fine. Gently fold in the blueberries.
4 Spoon the mixture into the muffin tin and bake for 25 minutes until risen and golden.

1 Purée the strawberries in a food processor or blender until smooth. Add the yogurt, icing sugar and vanilla extract and process briefly to mix everything together. Pour into a freezer-proof container. (The creamy strawberry mixture is also delicious eaten as it is.)
2 Freeze for 2 hours then remove from the freezer and whisk by hand to break up any ice crystals that have formed. Return to the freezer for another 2 hours then repeat the whisking process to break up any ice crystals. Return to the freezer again until solid.
3 Allow to soften in the fridge for 30 minutes before serving.

ENERGY-BOOSTING MUFFINS

The secret to good muffins is to not over-mix the batter – lumps are fine, which makes them a perfect introduction to cake-making for kids! A useful snack, these help to revive flagging energy levels by giving depleted blood-glucose levels a boost.

Makes 12
100g/1 stick butter, melted, plus extra
    for greasing
250g/2¼ cups plain flour
55g/½ cup wholemeal flour
175g/¾ cup unrefined caster sugar
1 tsp baking powder
½ tsp salt
284ml/1¼ cups buttermilk
2 eggs, beaten
150g/1 cup blueberries

BRAIN BOX

Blueberries are rich in powerful antioxidants called anthocyanidins. According to research, these help to mop up free radicals in both watery and fatty parts of the body, such as the brain. This is unusual in that many other antioxidants protect either the fatty or watery parts and not both.

APPLE & PLUM FLAPJACK PIE

Fruit crumble with a twist: this pie has a crisp nutty, oaty topping. You can vary the fruit base according to what's in season – rhubarb, nectarines, berries and pears are equally delicious. Dessert apples are used here instead of cooking apples, which need plenty of sugar to sweeten them.

Serves 4–6
3 dessert apples, cored, peeled and
    diced
squeeze of lemon juice
5 plums, halved, stoned and diced

for the topping:
4 tbsp golden syrup
75g/¾ stick unsalted butter
150g/¾ cup porridge oats
2 tbsp chopped hazelnuts
2 tbsp sunflower seeds

1 Preheat the oven to 180°C/350°F. Toss the apples in the lemon juice to prevent them browning and arrange in a 23 cm/9 in diameter ovenproof dish with the plums; stir well to combine.

2 To make the topping, melt the syrup and butter together in a heavy-based medium-sized saucepan over medium heat. Remove from the heat and stir in the oats, hazelnuts and seeds. Sprinkle the mixture over the top of the fruit. Bake for 20–25 minutes until golden and beginning to crisp.

DOUBLE-DECKER DATE BARS

These moist muesli-type bars contain a healthy dose of vitamins, minerals and essential fatty acids – they're incredibly moreish too!

Makes 16 squares
125g/1¼ sticks butter, cubed, plus
    extra for greasing
200g/1½ cups chopped dried dates
225ml/scant 1 cup water
125g/generous ½ cup porridge oats
115g/¾ cup light muscovado sugar
120g/1 cup wholemeal flour
1 tsp baking powder
2 tbsp sunflower seeds
40g/⅓ cup chopped mixed nuts

1 Preheat the oven to 180°C/350°F. Grease a 28 x 18 cm/11 x 7 in baking tin with the extra butter and line with baking parchment.
2 Put the dates and water in a saucepan and bring to the boil. Reduce the heat and simmer, half-covered, for 20 minutes until the dates are tender

BRAIN BOX

The brain needs a constant supply of glucose to function. Complex carbohydrates, supplied by the **wholemeal flour and oats** in this recipe, are the primary source of the brain's energy and also provide many nutrients too.

and mushy – most of the water should have been absorbed. Purée in a blender and set aside to cool.
3 Meanwhile, mix together the oats, sugar, flour, baking powder, seeds and chopped nuts in a large mixing bowl. Mix in the butter using your fingertips until the mixture is soft and crumbly.
4 Spoon three-quarters of the mixture into the prepared tin and press down with your fingers to make a firm, even layer. Spoon the date mixture over the oats. Sprinkle with the rest of the oat mixture and press down lightly.
5 Bake for 25 minutes until golden, then leave in the tin for 15 minutes to cool and firm up. Cut into 16 squares and remove from the tin.

BRAIN BOX

Apples are a good source of boron, which has been found to be important in maintaining mental alertness and concentration.

MINI FRUIT CRUMBLES

These pretty individual crumbles are perfect if you are just cooking for the children and want to make a small number of portions. They feature a nutritious combination of nectarines, oats and seeds. Don't use overripe fruit since it will collapse during cooking.

Serves 4
50g/½ stick unsalted butter, plus extra
   for greasing
4 nectarines, halved and stoned
100g/¾ cup wholemeal flour
2 tbsp porridge oats
1 tbsp sunflower seeds
4 tbsp demerara sugar

1 Preheat the oven to 180°C/350°F. Grease an ovenproof dish with the extra butter. Arrange the nectarines in the dish. Add a little water to the dish to prevent the fruit becoming dry.
2 Rub together the butter and flour with your fingertips until it forms coarse breadcrumbs. Stir in the oats, seeds and sugar then mix well.
3 Spoon the crumble mixture over the nectarine halves. Bake for 20 minutes or until the crumble is golden and slightly crisp.

COMFORT COOKIES

These American-style cookies are packed with nutritious oats, which help to steady blood levels, controlling mood swings and providing sustained amounts of energy – what more could you ask for!

Makes 10
125g/1¼ sticks unsalted butter
75g/½ cup light muscovado sugar
75g/⅓ cup self-raising flour
25g/¼ cup wholemeal self-raising
   flour
100g/½ cup whole porridge oats

1 Preheat the oven to 180°C/350°F. Line two baking sheets with baking parchment.
2 Beat together the butter and sugar in a mixing bowl until light and fluffy. Stir in both types of flour and the oats then mix well to make a soft dough.
3 Divide the dough into 10 pieces. Roll each piece into a ball and arrange on the baking sheets, well spaced out to allow room for the cookies to spread. Flatten the top of each ball slightly and bake for 15–20 minutes until just golden but still soft in the centre.
4 Leave to cool to 5 minutes then transfer to wire racks to cool further.

STRAWBERRY HAZELNUT SHORTBREADS

These melt-in-the-mouth shortbreads are topped with vanilla cream and juicy strawberries in this pretty dessert. You can store any leftover shortbreads in an airtight container.

Serves 6
100g/¾ cup plain flour
55g/½ cup wholemeal flour
40g/¼ cup fine oatmeal
1 tsp baking powder
pinch of salt
125g/1¼ sticks unsalted butter
4 tbsp golden caster sugar
50g/scant ½ cup finely chopped
   hazelnuts
1 tbsp milk

to serve:
125ml/½ cup double or whipping
   cream
1 tsp icing sugar
1 tsp natural vanilla extract
strawberries, halved if large

1 Preheat the oven to 180°C/350°F. Line two baking sheets with baking parchment.
2 Combine the two types of flour with the oatmeal, baking powder and salt in a large mixing bowl. Rub in the butter using your fingertips until the mixture resembles fine breadcrumbs. Stir in the sugar and chopped hazelnuts and then mix in the milk to form a soft dough.

3 Gently knead the dough into a ball and roll out on a lightly floured work surface. Using a 5 cm/2 in cutter, stamp out 12 rounds and arrange on the baking sheets, spaced well apart to allow the dough to spread.
4 Bake for 15 minutes until golden but still soft in the centre. Leave to cool for 5 minutes then transfer to a wire rack.
5 When the shortbread is cool and you are ready to serve, whip the cream with the icing sugar and vanilla extract until thickened. Place a shortbread on each serving plate, top with a good dollop of cream and arrange a few strawberries on top.

BRAIN BOX

Protein foods, like **hazelnuts and dairy produce**, are vital for building the brain's neurotransmitters or messengers.

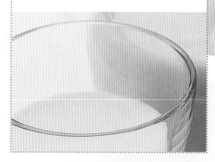

MERRY BERRY COBBLER

Berries are rich in antioxidants and vitamin C, vital for protecting the brain. Here, they are used as a base for a warming dessert that has a melt-in-the-mouth scone topping.

Serves 4
250g/2 cups mixed berries, such as
   raspberries, blackberries, blueberries,
   strawberries, defrosted if frozen
8 plums, halved, stoned and chopped
1 tsp cornflour
3 tbsp unrefined caster sugar

for the topping:
125g/1¼ sticks unsalted butter
2 tbsp unrefined caster sugar
200g/1¾ cups plain flour
2 tsp baking powder
2 tsp cornflour
1–2 tbsp single cream
demerara sugar, for sprinkling
   (optional)

1 Preheat the oven to 180°C/350°F. To prepare the fruit, put the berries and plums in a 20 x 25 cm/8 x 10 in dish. Mix the cornflour with a little water and add to the fruit with the sugar, stir until thoroughly combined.
2 To make the topping, beat the butter and sugar together until pale and fluffy. Mix in the flour, baking powder and cornflour. As the mixture becomes dry, stir in the cream to form a smooth soft dough.

This pudding contains a healthy dose of antioxidants, including the powerful anthocyanidins found particularly in **berries**. Antioxidants are vital for protecting the brain against unwanted toxins and free radicals.

3 Divide the dough into 8 balls, flatten each one slightly and arrange on top of the berry mixture. Sprinkle lightly with demerara sugar and bake for 20–25 minutes until the top is risen and golden.

BRAIN-BUSTING GINGERBREAD!

This rich teacake improves with age, becoming deliciously sticky and gooey. Molasses is much forgotten in baking, but is packed with beneficial minerals.

Makes 20 squares
150g/1½ sticks unsalted butter, plus
    extra for greasing
350g/3 cups self-raising flour
120g/1 cup wholemeal self-raising
    flour
3 tsp ground ginger
1 tsp bicarbonate of soda
60g/½ cup dried dates, chopped
275ml/generous 1 cup milk
1 egg, beaten
225g/1 cup light muscovado sugar
125g/⅓ cup molasses
175g/½ cup golden syrup

1 Preheat the oven to 180°C/350°F. Grease a 20 cm/8 in square cake tin with the extra butter and line the base with baking parchment.
2 Sift both types of flour, adding any bran left in the sieve, into a large mixing bowl. Stir in the ginger, bicarbonate of soda and dates. Beat together the milk and egg and set aside.
3 Put the sugar, molasses, syrup and butter in a saucepan, and heat, stirring, over a medium-low heat until melted together. Pour the mixture into the dry ingredients with the milk and egg then beat until smooth.

4 Pour the mixture into the cake tin. Level the top with the back of a spoon and bake for 55–60 minutes until a skewer inserted into the middle comes out clean. Leave the cake in the tin for 10 minutes then turn out on to a wire rack to cool completely. Peel off the baking parchment.

Just one tablespoon of **molasses** contains more calcium than a glass of milk, plus plenty of iron, all the B vitamins, magnesium and manganese – a super brain food. This thick, almost black syrup can be found in health food shops and the health food section of many large supermarkets.

NUTTY APPLE CRUNCH

Another speedy low-fat version of crumble, this healthy hazelnut-topped apple purée is delicious hot or cold.

Serves 4
8 dessert apples, peeled, cored and
   roughly diced

for the topping:
2 slices wholemeal bread, crusts
   removed
25g/¼ stick unsalted butter
40g/⅓ cup chopped toasted hazelnuts
3 tbsp light muscovado sugar
1 tsp ground cinnamon

1 Process the bread in a food processor to make breadcrumbs. Melt the butter in a frying pan and add the breadcrumbs, hazelnuts and sugar and cook, stirring frequently, for 3 minutes or until golden and crisp. Stir in the cinnamon and set aside.
2 Meanwhile, place the apples in a non-metallic saucepan with 2 tablespoons of water. Cook, half-covered, over a medium-low heat for 10 minutes or until very tender. Mash with a fork to break down the apples to a rough purée.
3 Sprinkle some of the hazelnut mixture into the bottom of 4 ramekin dishes, top with the apple and then the rest of the hazelnut mixture. Serve at once.

MINI PEACH TARTS

Fantastically simple, these attractive little tarts can be filled with the fruit of your choice – apples, pears, blackberries and nectarines all work well – and they are a good way of encouraging little ones to eat more of the fresh stuff.

Makes 6
3 ripe peaches
375g/13oz ready-rolled puff pastry
1 egg, separated
6 tbsp fresh custard
1 tbsp unrefined caster sugar, for
   sprinkling

1 Preheat the oven to 200°C/400°F. Line a large baking sheet with baking parchment.
2 Put the peaches in a large bowl, cover with boiling water and leave for 30 seconds. Remove from the water with a slotted spoon and, when cool enough to handle, peel off the skins. Cut each peach into quarters and remove the stone, then slice.
3 Lay out the pastry and cut six 8 cm/3¼ in diameter circles. Arrange the pastry rounds on the baking sheet and brush with egg white. Spoon 1 tablespoon of custard in the centre of each pastry round, leaving a 2 cm/¾ in border.

4 Fold in the edges of the pastry to encase the custard and brush the pastry with the egg yolk. Arrange the slices of peach on top of the custard and sprinkle with a little sugar. Bake for 15 minutes until the pastry is risen and golden.

MANGO FOOL

'Fool' is perhaps the wrong name for this creamy dessert since its vitamin and mineral content can actually aid mental clarity and alertness.

Serves 4
1 large mango, stoned, peeled and
  roughly chopped
200ml/scant 1 cup whipping cream
2 tsp unrefined icing sugar
4 tbsp natural bio yogurt

1 Place the mango in a food processor or blender, reserving four slices for decoration. Purée the mango until smooth.
2 Add the cream, sugar and yogurt and blend until combined.
3 Spoon the mixture into 4 glasses and refrigerate for 1 hour to firm up slightly. Decorate each glass with a mango slice before serving.

BRAIN BOX

Although **cream** should be treated as a special occasion food and therefore not eaten every day because of its high fat content, it does provide essential protein, calcium, tryptophan and B-group vitamins.

LEMON PUDDINGS

Intensely lemony, these puddings develop a light sponge topping and a curd-like sauce at the bottom during baking. Citrus fruits are often waxed, which acts as a preservative, so make sure you buy unwaxed fruit or, if you can't find unwaxed fruit, scrub the skins with washing-up liquid and rinse well.

Makes 6
50g/½ stick unsalted butter, plus extra
  for greasing
100g/scant ½ cup unrefined caster
  sugar
finely grated zest and juice of
  2 unwaxed lemons
3 eggs, separated
100ml/scant ½ cup milk
40g/scant 1½ cup self-raising flour

1 Preheat the oven to 180°C/350°F. Lightly grease 6 ramekin dishes with the extra butter.
2 Using a hand whisk or electric mixer, beat together the butter and sugar until pale and smooth. Gradually beat in the lemon zest and juice – the mixture will look curdled but this is not a problem.
3 Beat in the egg yolks, one at a time then stir in the milk and flour.
4 Whisk the egg whites in a clean, grease-free bowl until soft peaks form. Fold the egg whites into the lemon mixture until evenly incorporated. Pour

---

the mixture into the ramekins and place the ramekins in a baking tin.
5 Pour enough hot water into the baking tin to come halfway up the sides of the ramekins and bake for 25 minutes or until the puddings have risen and the tops are golden.

BRAIN BOX

Iron is found in useful amounts in **eggs**. This mineral is crucial for healthy brain function and a lack of iron has been linked to poor concentration and depression.

PEAR CUSTARD PUDDING

This light custard dessert is similar to clafoutis, the French batter pudding, and is especially delicious served warm.

Serves 4–6
butter, for greasing
6 tbsp unrefined caster sugar
2 ripe pears, peeled, cored and sliced
juice of ½ lemon
4 free-range eggs
300ml/1¼ cups single cream
300ml/1¼ cups full-cream milk
pinch of salt
55g/½ cup plain flour

1 Preheat the oven to 200°C/400°F. Lightly grease a 20 cm/8 in diameter baking or flan dish and sprinkle the base with 1 tablespoon of the sugar.
2 Dip the sliced pears in the lemon juice to prevent them browning and arrange them in the dish.
3 Put the eggs, cream, milk, salt, flour and remaining caster sugar in a food processor and process until smooth and frothy. Pour this over the pears.
4 Bake for 30–35 minutes, until golden – the custard should still be quite wobbly, but it will firm up as it cools. Serve warm.

VARIATION
To make cherry custard pudding, the classic version of this dessert, replace the pears with 20 fresh, ripe pitted cherries. For other variations, you could replace the pears with 2 dessert apples, peeled cored and sliced, or 4 plums, halved and stoned, or 2 peaches, stoned and sliced.

BRAIN BOX

Calcium and B-group vitamins are found in plentiful amounts in **milk and dairy products** in general. They also contain tryptophan, which is said to aid the production of serotonin in the brain, a calming and mood-lifting chemical.

DELICIOUS DRINKS

Hydration is just as important for concentration and clarity of thought as food. Easy to make, these drinks are great alternatives to shop-bought high-sugar drinks – and they are tasty, too!

MANGO & BANANA SMOOTHIE

Taste the tropics with this energy-boosting thick smoothie. Nectarines, peaches or plums make flavourful alternatives.

Serves 3–4
1 large mango, peeled, stoned and
    roughly chopped
2–3 bananas, sliced
125ml/½ cup natural live yogurt
250ml/1 cup milk

1 Place the mango, bananas, yogurt and milk in a food processor or blender and process until smooth and creamy.

BRAIN BOX

Bananas are rich in potassium, which is vital for conducting nerve impulses in the brain.

Live bio yogurt is high in mind-boosting protein and also promotes healthy digestion and assimilation of nutrients.

BANANARAMA

Filling and substantial – the perfect protein-boosting drink to fight flagging energy levels. Serve alongside wholemeal toast or a muffin.

Serves 2
2 bananas, thickly sliced
1 tbsp smooth peanut butter
125ml/½ cup natural bio yogurt
300ml/1¼ cups milk
½ tsp ground cinnamon

1 Place the bananas, peanut butter, yogurt, milk and cinnamon in a blender. Process until smooth, thick and frothy.

PEACH MELBA SMOOTHIE

A liquid version of the classic pudding, which provides plentiful amounts of vitamins and minerals as well as mind-stimulating protein.

Serves 2–3
3 nectarines, peeled, stoned and
    roughly chopped
150g/5½oz raspberries
500ml/2 cups milk
3 decent scoops of good quality vanilla
    ice cream

1 Place the nectarines, raspberries, milk and ice cream in a food processor or blender and process until smooth.

BRAIN BOX

Raspberries are one of the few fresh fruits to contain iron as well as B-group vitamins and vitamin C. Maintaining iron levels is crucial for learning, while vitamin C helps the absorption of the mineral when consumed at the same time. Berries also contain the potent antioxidants anthocyanidins.

Oranges and pineapples contain some vitamin B1 (thiamine) which helps to convert carbohydrates into energy and is important for memory and concentration. Carotenoids and vitamin C work together to fight free radicals.

SUPER JUICE

Kids who start the day with this nutrient-rich juice as part of their breakfast will give their memory and energy levels a vital boost. If served with eggs, the vitamin C in the juice will aid the absorption of iron found in the eggs.

Serves 4
1 small mango, peeled, stoned and
   roughly chopped
1 small pineapple, peeled, cored and
   roughly chopped
400ml/1⅔ cups freshly squeezed
   orange juice

1 Put the mango and pineapple through a juicer and combine with the fresh orange juice. Serve immediately to ensure minimum loss of vitamins, which are depleted when cut fruit is exposed to the air.

POWER JUICE

Freshly squeezed fruit and vegetable combinations are an excellent way of encouraging children to eat up their veg and giving them a vitamin boost at the same time.

Serves 2
4 apples, cored
2 large carrots, peeled
handful seedless grapes

1 Put the apples, carrots and grapes through a juicer. Taste and dilute with a little water if too strong then divide between 2 glasses and serve immediately.

ORANGE FIZZ

Ditch the sugar- and caffeine-laden carbonated drinks for this refreshing citrus vitamin C-rich alternative.

Serves 4
4 oranges
2 tbsp lemon juice
carbonated mineral water

1 Squeeze the oranges. Combine the orange juice and lemon juice in a jug and divide between four glasses. Top up with fizzy water before serving.

Anxiety and stress increase levels of free radicals in the body, which can deplete brain energy. Antioxidants found in **fresh fruit and vegetables** combat the harmful affects of these free radicals. In addition, the boron found in **apples** helps to encourage positive thinking.

COCONUT & MANGO SMOOTHIE

This smoothie is similar to an Indian sweet lassi and is surprisingly filling. It is a perfect summer drink.

Serves 4
1 large mango, peeled and chopped
400g/14oz can half-fat coconut milk
250ml/1 cup thick natural yogurt
125ml/½ cup milk
2 tbsp soft light brown sugar
1 tsp ground cinnamon

1 Place the mango, coconut milk, yogurt, milk, sugar and half the cinnamon in a food processor or blender. Process until smooth and frothy. Pour into 4 glasses and add a few ice cubes. Sprinkle with the remaining cinnamon just before serving.

VARIATION
Coconut & Banana Smoothie Replace the mango with 1 large banana for an equally delicious smoothie.

BRAIN BOX

Yogurt is a good source of the amino acid tyrosine, which is converted in the brain to noradrenaline and has the effect of increasing motivation and alertness. It also provides beneficial amounts of the calming magnesium, calcium and B-group vitamins.

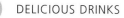

LEMON BARLEY WATER

A children's classic, this drink does contain some sugar, but in much lower amounts than the shop-bought versions. What's more it's richer in vitamin C. Make sure you use unwaxed lemons since citrus fruit are commonly waxed, which acts as a preservative.

About 10 servings
225g/1 cup pearl barley
1.75 litres/7 cups water
grated rind of 1 unwaxed lemon
juice of 3 lemons
50g/1¼ cups unrefined caster sugar

1 Rinse the pearl barley under cold running water then place in a large saucepan. Cover with the water and bring to the boil. Reduce the heat and simmer gently for 20 minutes, skimming off any froth that rises to the surface. Remove the pan from the heat.
2 Add the lemon rind and sugar to the pan, stir well until the sugar has dissolved and leave to cool. Strain, discarding the pearl barley, and add the lemon juice to the liquid.
3 Taste for sweetness and add more sugar if necessary. Chill before serving.

STRAWBERRIES & CREAM SMOOTHIE

This thick and creamy shake is substantial enough to make a filling breakfast if accompanied by toast. You could opt for natural bio yogurt instead of vanilla ice cream, which would reduce the fat and sugar levels. Prepare just before serving for optimum nutrient levels.

Serves 3–4
300g/2 cups strawberries, halved if large
300ml/1¼ cups milk
½ tsp natural vanilla extract
3 decent scoops of good-quality vanilla ice cream

BRAIN BOX

Milk is a complete protein, meaning that it contains all eight essential amino acids, one of which is the brain-stimulating tyrosine.

Strawberries are a good source of vitamin C, carotenoids and some B-group vitamins.

1 Place the strawberries in a food processor or blender and process until puréed. Add the milk, vanilla and ice cream and process until thick and creamy.

HONEY BERRY FIZZ

This low-sugar version of the popular blackcurrant cordial can be diluted with still or fizzy water but the latter always goes down well. The bags of frozen mixed red berries you can buy in supermarkets are ideal for this.

Serves 4
200g/7oz frozen fruits of the forest, including a mixture of fruit such as blackberries, raspberries, blackcurrants and strawberries
2 tbsp runny honey
carbonated or still water, to serve

1 Place the berries and honey in a saucepan and gently heat through, stirring occasionally, until the fruit has defrosted and is very juicy. Transfer to a blender and process until fairly smooth.
2 To remove any pips in the fruit, press the mixture through a sieve into a bowl and discard the pulp and seeds. Pour the juice into a jug. Leave to cool then refrigerate, covered, until ready to serve. To serve, half fill a glass with the berry juice and top with water.

BRAIN BOX

Dehydration can affect behaviour leading to poor concentration, tiredness and depression. It is vital for children to drink enough **fluids** throughout the day to help with mental energy.

BRAIN BOX

The calcium and magnesium found in **milk** are known as nature's tranquillisers, which is why they make such good bedtime drinks.

Almonds are also rich in these minerals as well as memory-boosting B vitamins, omega-6 essential fatty acids and zinc.

USE-YOUR-NUT SHAKE

A hint of chocolate adds to the popularity of this wholesome frothy milk shake.

Serves 2
40g/¼ cup sliced almonds
2 bananas, thickly sliced
300ml/1¼ cups milk
2 tbsp good quality drinking chocolate powder

1 Grind the almonds in a blender until finely ground and smooth. Add the bananas, milk and chocolate powder then blend until smooth and frothy.

REAL HOT CHOCOLATE

A real calming treat at the end of the day – why use powdered cocoa when you can enjoy the real thing?

Serves 1
250ml/1 cup milk
20–25g/¾–1oz dark chocolate, broken (plus grated chocolate to decorate)
½ tsp maple syrup

1 Gently heat the milk in a small saucepan.
2 Break the chocolate into the milk and whisk until the chocolate has melted and the milk is frothy.
3 Pour into a mug and stir in the maple syrup. Decorate with a little grated chocolate and serve.

INDEX

ACKNOWLEDGMENTS

The author would like to thank the following people and institutions for their help, advice and assistance during the research of this book:

Tony Steer at Human Nutrition Research
Professor Peter Rogers, Psychology Head of Department, University of Bristol
Professor David Benton, Department of Psychology, University of Swansea
Beth Arkinstall, Senior Dietician, Bristol Children's Hospital
The Institute of Optimum Nutrition

Carroll & Brown Publishers would like to thank:

Production Manager Karol Davies
Computer Management Paul Stradling
Photographer's Assistant David Yems
Food Preparation Lizzie Harris
Indexer Caroline Smith

The photograph of the farmers' market on page 32 by Gareth Jones
was supplied by courtesy of
FARMA, The National Farmers' Retail & Markets Association,
The Greenhouse, P O Box 575, Southampton SO15 7BZ
Telephone 0845 230 2150